The Family *Blessing* Initiative

Revival @ Home

52 Days of Prayer
for the
Rebuilding of Your Family Walls

Val & Brenda Dodd
Diane Roblin-Lee

Library and Archives Canada Cataloguing in Publication

Dodd, Val
    The family blessing initiative : 52 days of prayer for the
restoration of your family / Val & Brenda Dodd, Diane Roblin-Lee.

Includes bibliographical references.
ISBN 978-1-896213-72-9

    1. Families--Religious aspects--Christianity. 2. Families--Religious life.
3. Prayer. 4. Christian life. I. Dodd, Brenda II. Roblin-Lee, Diane, 1945-
III. Title.

BV4526.3.D64 2013   248.8'45   C2013-900057-7

Copyright 2013—Brenda Dodd and Diane Roblin-Lee
Published by byDesign Media www.bydesignmedia.ca
Layout & Design—Diane Roblin-Lee
Cover—Diane Roblin-Lee
Editor— Stephanie Nickel

byDesign
MEDIA

There is a cry echoing, reverberating through the universe...

"Do something!"

"If you do away with the yoke of oppression,
with the pointing finger and malicious talk,
and if you spend yourselves in behalf of the hungry
and satisfy the needs of the oppressed,
then your light will rise in the darkness,
and your night will become like the noonday.
The LORD will guide you always;
He will satisfy your needs in a sun-scorched land
and will strengthen your frame.
You will be like a well-watered garden,
like a spring whose waters never fail.
Your people will rebuild the ancient ruins
and will raise up the age-old foundations;
you will be called Repairer of Broken Walls,
Restorer of Streets with Dwellings."

(Isaiah 58:9-12)

Contents

Purpose ~ by Rev. Val Dodd 6

Foreword ~ by David Mainse 7

1. Why a Family Blessing Initiative? 9

2. Cues From Nehemiah 23

3. Taking Up Our Positions 49
   ~ Homeland Security
   ~ Legacy Security
   ~ Cyber Security

4. My/Our Greatest Hopes 57

5. Ready to Begin ~ Prayer 59

6. Fifty-Two Days of Promises, Prayer
   and Proclamations Over Your Family 62

7. Summary of Changes I've Seen 166

8. Dedication & Celebration 169

9. Pages for Recording God's Ongoing Work
   in Your Family 171

Postlogue and Contact 199

Purpose

As I (Val) was praying one morning, I had a download from Heaven about Nehemiah rebuilding the walls of Jerusalem in 52 days. I heard the LORD say (Jesus said His sheep know His voice!) "If people will pray a blessing for 52 days over their families and homes, I will restore them and help them to rebuild their homes."

Nehemiah, whose name means Comforter, Consoler, is a picture of the Holy Spirit, who has come to repair, rebuild and restore. Just as Nehemiah came to rebuild the walls around Jerusalem, so the Holy Spirit will help us rebuild and restore the walls of our homes.

The purpose of this book is to restore family unity, to help rebuild the prayer walls of your home.

Nehemiah 4:14 says, *"Don't be afraid, remember the LORD, who is great and awesome, and fight for your brothers, your sons, and your daughters, your wives, and your homes."*

Rev. Val Dodd
C.E.O., Singing Waters Ministries

Foreword

Rev. Val Dodd is a hero of mine! Throughout his years working with *100 Huntley Street*, he showed himself to be a man of God, proving his call to ministry by compassion, determination, sacrifice and excellent results in all his initiatives. He refused ever to give up on a person to whom he was ministering. Now, he is showing the same qualities in taking on the challenge of building and strengthening entire families. He's cheering us on from his place in Heaven since his graduation from this life. This book is a most precious and practical gift that he has left behind for us all. I will be forever grateful for the ministry of my dear, dear friend Val!

David Mainse
Founder—Crossroads Christian Communications Inc.

The Family Blessing Initiative

*is not about "trying" something new;
it is about engaging Someone
who is "tried and true"
to restore our families.*

The Family Altar
will alter your family.

1

Why a Family Blessing Initiative?

"I never see my kids anymore—it's like they don't care about our family..."

"Mom just doesn't get it—she expects us to be the Brady bunch, but Jack will never be my dad..."

"My daughter was taken into custody last night. Drugs. She won't talk to me. Look—with three kids to feed, a husband who's been laid off and my two jobs, I just can't do it anymore..."

We hear comments like the above all the time. Families are in crisis. It breaks our hearts. Not one of us can claim immunity from the brokenness that has marred at least 50 percent of homes.

There is a cry echoing, reverberating through the universe: "Do something!"

Recuperating from major surgery in October of 2010, I (Val) awoke one morning with the recurring thought, "Bring the family back to the table." I couldn't shake it. It was as though the thought was being implanted in my heart and mind. I sensed it was being given within the context of restoring the family altar.

Just one month earlier, God had begun to impress a new message on my heart. It was to be called "Revival @ Home."

Revival at home. How was I supposed to have a heart for ministering to families when I had so recently lost my eldest son? Craig had died suddenly from an undiagnosed condition at the age of 37 and, in losing him, I had lost one of the most precious parts of my life. My enthusiasm for family ministry had withered in my grief.

But now—God seemed to be bringing a fresh calling in the very place my wife, Brenda, and I had suffered such loss. I began to sharpen my spiritual antenna for further direction. Our son Jason (my associate pastor at the time) alerted me to a book called *Church + Home* by Mark Holmen. What I read in that book underscored the importance of strengthening Christian families and deepened my sense of God's fresh call on my life.

Now, looking back over the past two years and seeing how God has assembled the pieces of this call, and because of its purpose, I believe this is the most important assignment the LORD has ever entrusted to me.

Prior to my 2010 surgery, Brenda and I had been talking about the negative results the loss of prayer in homes has had on individual families and on our culture in general.

Point of Change

Twenty years ago, Canadian courts ruled that the LORD's Prayer could not be said in public schools, contending that it constituted religious indoctrination. Since then, the continuous efforts to scrub every vestige of Christianity from schools have resulted in huge cultural changes in homes.

For me (Diane), as for countless others, this was a devastating blow. At the time when Secular Humanism was weaseling its way into our public education system (masquerading as a non-partisan, philosophy), the LORD awakened me to its anti-God roots. Heavily burdened for our children, I battled its influence in the public-school system through a movement we called "EduAction." People needed to be made aware that Secular Humanism was not to be confused with the "humanitarianism" they assumed it to be. Secular Humanism had been recognized by the U.S. courts as a religion in 1933. It was established entirely on the religion of atheism and had absolutely nothing to do with humanitarianism. Now it was threatening to overtake the hearts and minds of our unsuspecting students and teachers.

Running for a provincial seat gave me a voice in the election debates—but most people didn't want to know about threats to the Christian foundations of our society. During a heated battle in a P.T.A. meeting, a woman, fed-up with something she didn't want to understand, said, "Oh Diane, don't you think you'd have more support if anybody was really interested."

And so, despite enormous efforts by many others who were not blinded to the frontal assault on the foundational beliefs of our country, the spirit of atheism invaded our schools and society. Within a few short years, prayer in schools was outlawed and we began to see the decline in our culture and values.

Likewise, in the United States, moral decline rapidly accelerated following the June 25, 1962, U.S. Supreme Court's removal of prayer from schools. The message the schools sent to the populace was that it was okay to remove God from His rightful place.

Since that time, North American life has experienced a radical decline in the culture of youth, family, education and patriotism. Our once orderly society, based on the family as the basic building block, has become the chaotic "everything goes" arena in which we find ourselves today. Many homes are in desperate turmoil. Worried parents wring their hands, not knowing what to do.

Seldom, anymore, does a tree-lined street guarantee a whole row of two-parent families where the generations appreciate and respect one another. Instead, many one-parent families struggle to keep food on the table and the lights on. It's not unusual to find seniors entirely forsaken by children and grandchildren who are too self-absorbed to show them love, while other seniors feel the uncomfortable weight of being a burden on middle-aged children, sandwiched between their care and a myriad of other responsibilities. With bitterness, many remember the days before relationships went wrong, when days were happier, necessities were adequate and their family name was respected.

Where families used to be thought of as 'safe havens' from the pressures of the outside world, many have become sparring rings where members accuse each other of being responsible for their inadequacies, past and present. Confusion, bitterness, battery, exhaustion and shame have replaced the aromas of apple pie and emotional security.

About 20 years after the removal of prayer from schools, Specialty Research Associates, under the direction of David Barton, released a report titled *America: To Pray or Not to*

Pray[1]. While this was an American report, the phenomenon was reflected in Canada. To our knowledge, it is the most comprehensive, definitive study on the subject. A few of its findings showed that over the 20 years, there was:

1. A 187 percent increase in teen pregnancies for girls aged 15–19

2. A 553 percent increase in teen pregnancies for girls aged 10–14

3. A 226 percent increase in sexually transmitted diseases in the first 12 years following the removal of prayer from schools

4. A 300 percent increase in divorce *each year* for the first 15 years following the removal of prayer from schools

5. A 353 percent increase in unmarried people living together

6. A 160 percent increase in single parent families

7. An increase of 544 percent in violent crime

8. An increase of 1,375 percent in illegal drug use

9. Student suicides went from ranking 12th as the cause of death among young people to 3rd by 1990

10. SAT scores declined for 18 consecutive years following the removal of prayer from schools.

Until 1967, there were no recorded abortions in Canada, because they were illegal. In 1968 when Morgantaler started the big business of abortion, there were 106 recorded. By 2000, there were 105,642. In 2010, they stopped keeping count.

1. David Barton, *America to Pray? or Not to Pray?* (Aledo, Texas Wallbuilder Press, 1994).

In the years since the Specialty Research Associates report, the advent of the Internet has seen pornography and sex slavery become two of the most lucrative businesses in the world.

Illegal drugs have become an enormous and uncontrollable problem. Illicit sex and violence have become commonplace. In many families, children have adopted the "new attitude" and turned their backs on whatever diligent parents have tried to teach them, flaunting an arrogance generally foreign to the preceding generations.

Beyond the most dramatic stresses, other factors like high-pressure sports, the isolationist communication of new technologies, body image issues, occult influences through popular movies and children's programming and uncertainty in the economy impose themselves upon us. Is it any wonder teen and childhood suicides have become epidemic?

And who has the strength to resist the brilliant Madison Avenue advertisers who want not only people's wallets but the hearts and loyalty of their children? They dictate everything from the clothes and shoes our children wear to the food they eat, molding their minds to the spirit of this age. Shopping, even for the cash-strapped, has become a form of entertainment, an all-consuming sport. Genesis chapters two and three tell about Adam and Eve lusting after the enticing fruit of the tree of the knowledge of good and evil rather than on the tree of life. 1 John 2:16 says, *"For everything in the world—the lust of the flesh, the lust of the eyes, and the pride of life—comes not from the Father but from the world."*
Is this lust for self-gratification not what is driving many people today?

Some provinces have begun implementing social engineering in our schools by teaching a "new" sexuality, morality and theology, not bothering to admit it's nothing but the old *immorality*. This spirit of immorality brings with it a spirit of lawlessness by keeping parents' values out of the classroom. Parents who protest are viewed as intrusive throwbacks. They have never faced such monumental attacks on their families.

What is really going on here?

Carle Zimmerman, a Harvard sociologist, wrote a classic in 1947, *Family and Civilization*[2], a study on 3,000 years of tribal and cultural rites in families. It is a compelling portrait of the morphing of families throughout history, from the solidarity of tribal clans, which he called Trustee families, to today's untethered Atomist model, where people do whatever feels good. The happiness of the individual trumps societal norms and, in the name of tolerance, individual rights become lost in the demands for the greater good.

People now over the age of 35 were raised in the preceding Domestic (his term) era, where father and mother, government and laws, provided the most generally accepted framework.

The transition from Domestic to Atomic has been swift and confusing. What is now accepted as normal, would have shocked our grandparents. Zimmerman's work helps to clear the fog allowing us to see why things are changing.

People raised in the Domestic era find it very difficult to understand the thinking of the new, Atomic, generation. Last week, there was an article in the paper about adultery being "the new norm." Anyone who has even read the Ten Commandments knows adultery was an absolute no-no to God and so sees this as a huge cause for concern.

For Christians, the not-so-subtle attack on their value system

2.   Carle Zimmerman, *Family and Civilization*
      (ISBN 978-1933859378) 1947.

(which is based on the eternal Word of God) is a stab in the carotid artery of their families. The life-blood of their value system runs directly through the precepts, principles and guidelines of God.

Many people of the Domestic era are wondering what's going on. They need to get clarity and wake up to the root of what's happening in their families. It's not an isolated problem; it's a sign of the times—evidence of a stage of cultural decline.

But signs of the times can point the way for our families only if we allow it. That doesn't mean we stick our heads in the sand and ignore "progress;" it means standing strong on the Word of God, using the wisdom He gives us and making progress work for us, instead of against us. For instance, it means harnessing the Internet for our purposes and moving ahead positively in the Spirit of God rather than being dragged along, kicking and screaming, by the spirit of the times, getting sucked into worrying about the mountain of evil we can't flatten. We must take leadership in our families and experience the "Revival @ Home."

Zimmerman gave a prophetic warning to society regarding the signs of cultural decline. A few of these are:

- Increased and rapid "causeless" divorce
- Decreased number of children, population decay, and increased public disrespect of parents and parenthood
- Elimination of the real meaning of the marriage ceremony
- Popularity of pessimistic doctrines about the early heroes
- Rise of theories that companionate marriage or a permissible looser family form would solve the problem

Performing a mental checklist of Zimmerman's warnings, in relation to today's society, gives a clear picture of where we are in terms of cultural decline. It sounds a lot like the picture of the last days in 2 Timothy 1-4:

"There will be terrible times in the last days. People will be lovers of themselves, lovers of money, boastful, proud, abusive, disobedient to their parents, ungrateful, unholy, without love, unforgiving, slanderous, without self-control, brutal, not lovers of the good, treacherous, rash, conceited, lovers of pleasure rather than lovers of God."

One of the saddest stories about families in the Old Testament is found in Judges 2:9-11, where it tells of Joshua and the following generations of Israelites: *"And they buried him within the border of his inheritance at Timnath Heres, in the mountains of Ephraim, on the north side of Mount Gaash. When all that generation had been gathered to their fathers, another generation arose after them who did not know the LORD nor the work which He had done for Israel. Then the children of Israel did evil in the sight of the LORD, and served the Baals..."*

The popular culture today is a mirror of that generation which *"did not know the LORD or the work which He has done.... Then the children...did evil in the sight of the LORD...."* It's a result of families neglecting to pass on the knowledge of God to the oncoming generations.

Getting a grip on the importance of restoring families and establishing a way of going before God together is foundational. It has been traditionally called the "family altar." When parents take up their positions as priests and ministers of the home, things gradually begin to be set right in families, because, when we align ourselves with God He responds.

Despite the present circumstances of our society, God said, *"I will never leave you or forsake you"* (Joshua 1:5; Hebrews 13:5) and *"I am with you always to the very ends of the age"* (Matthew 28:20). Obviously, despite the tumult of the times, we are not alone. God is still with us.

What's the Answer?

We wondered what we could possibly do to alleviate the overwhelming situations in so many homes. It was obvious that working to return formal prayer to the schools at this juncture would be not only futile but unwise. Multiculturalism dictates the fact that if we were to try to reintroduce corporate prayer in schools, it would have to be a benign civil-religious prayer that satisfies everyone and offends no one. What is that? It would be crazy to suggest that such a caricature of true prayer could ever serve a meaningful purpose.

Was there nothing we could do to change the course of society and bring restoration to beleaguered families?

Thinking further, we realized that government can never truly take prayer out of schools. Why? Because children who have been taught to pray in their homes take the ability to pray with them—in their hearts. If they can pray in groups, whether silently or aloud, so much the better, but no one needs a legislated ritual to pray. All that is needed is a sincere and trusting heart that knows God will hear and answer prayer, no matter the circumstances. If parents teach their children to pray, many of the adverse developments in society can be reversed, or at least alleviated. Teaching children throughout the world to pray, whether at school or at home, is doable. Rather than fussing over a ship that has already sailed, we can board another vessel.

The spontaneous thought I (Val) had that October morning in 2010 felt like an answer. Could it be the direction from God we had been seeking? Prayer might have been legislated out of schools, but homes are another issue. If prayer *has* been removed from our homes, we have only ourselves to blame.

A few months after God's initial nudge with regard to family ministry, Brenda and I went to Florida for a couple of weeks. One day, in a grocery store, I was perusing a recipe rack. A card caught my eye. It said, "Bring your family back to the table." A few weeks later, I saw an Uncle Ben's commercial that began with "Bring your family to the table...." I thought of the scripture that promises confirmation of God's Word and had a strong feeling that these were, in fact, nudges of His confirmation. It was seeming more and more as though the reminders of my recurring thought were indicators of divine direction.

Increasingly, God began to speak to me about families communicating and how to turn those conversations into godly communications (prayer). I knew He was giving me a strong mandate to lead families into a restoration of the family prayer time. Only supernatural intervention through prayer could turn the tide on the tsunami of destruction that was well on its way to destroying the basic unit of society.

I began to think about the revivals of the past century, especially the one in Wales in 1904-1905, where the Holy Spirit fell on a young Welshman named Evan Roberts and a group of young people. During the spring of 1904, Roberts was repeatedly awakened at 1:00 a.m. and met with God until 5:00 a.m. The great Welsh revival followed. It was a divine intervention that drastically altered life in every area of society.

Families were forever changed. God came in His power and transformed whole towns. Most of the shady establishments simply disappeared; crime fell and jails were essentially emptied. It was reported that, because the police had not much to do, they formed singing quartets. While Evan Roberts was the spark God used to change society, there was no real human leader of the revival—and no one was more conscious of that fact than Evan himself. He said, "This movement is not of me, it is of God. I would not dare direct it...it is the Spirit alone, which is leading us."[3]

We serve the same God as Evan Roberts. If God could change filthy-talking, brothel-frequenting, wife-beating, mean-spirited family members at the turn of the 20th Century, why could He not change alcoholic, drug-stupored, techno-freak, porn-addicted, atheistic family members at the turn of *this* century? If He could mend broken hearts, bodies and spirits *then*, why not *now?* The simple answer is, "He can."

The Home as a Sanctuary

Spiritual life in the 21st century is largely centered around the church. That needs to change. The church should be an extension of our homes—not the other way around. Spiritual life needs to define our homes as sanctuaries of love, safety, belonging, trust and godly instruction. When there is unity in our homes, our churches will be strong.

We expect schools to teach our kids math and church to teach them how to pray. Paid professionals relieve us of our responsibilities to "grow" our kids and shape our families.

The way we have approached church growth and development has resulted in fine church members, the grooming of

3. Ellis, *Living Echoes*, Delyn Press.

wonderful church leaders and pride in excellent organizations, but we haven't done the job of making people great leaders *in their homes*.

This is very different from the perspective of the early church.

Dowgeiwicz writes, "Judaism survived persecution in every generation because the real structure and function of religious life was home centered. Although so many synagogues were destroyed over the course of centuries, Judaism survived because every Jew was expected to be knowledgeable about the faith of his ancestors. Therefore Judaism could always survive in the home. The home was a little sanctuary, a *miqdash meyat*, to be set aside for the worship of God, the study of His Word, and a place of hospitality."[4]

In the early 2000's, our church incorporated a blessing of the sons and daughters into our ministry. It was a "Barbarakah"[5] (like a Christian Bar Mitzvah). We shared this with a number of churches who found it to be a practical and sound way of helping build the lives of young people.

Even at that time, I (Val) had begun to think about the home as a sanctuary. Acts 2:46 speaks of breaking bread together in the home. In their book *Recovery of Family Life*[6] Pauline and Elton Trueblood say, " If we can believe that a home is potentially as much a sanctuary as any ecclesiastical building can ever be, we are well on the way to the recovery of family life—which our generation sorely needs."

The family is the place where parents and children should learn to put others' needs before their own desires, to love sac-

---

4. Eusebius, *Ecclesiastical History*, Popular Edition, Grand Rapids: Baker Book House, 1973, p. 186-187.
5. Adopted with the permission of Craig Hill from his book, *Ancient Paths*.
6. Trueblood, Elton and Pauline, The Recovery of Family Life, New York: Harper & Bros., 1953, p. 120.

rificially for the welfare and protection of the whole family. As these qualities are nurtured, they translate into a civic-minded approach to life as the child matures, contributing to a caring society. If a consciousness for living sacrificially within a family group doesn't happen, it may not happen at all—leading to a community of self-absorbed isolationists, texting the person beside them.

Second Corinthians 5:20 says, *"We are therefore Christ's ambassadors, as though God were making his appeal through us. We implore you on Christ's behalf: be reconciled to God."*

If we truly are ambassadors for Christ, then every Christian home should be an embassy for the Kingdom of God and a prophetic witness to God's love by restoring His blessings—a *sanctuary* of His grace.

As the Church, we need to help fathers and mothers reverse the moral decline and the deconstruction of our Christian and family values by strengthening the family and encouraging it to return to the table—whatever form that table may take.

The Shema (A declaration of faith in our one God)

Deuteronomy 6:4-10: *"Hear, O Israel: The LORD our God, the LORD is one! You shall love the LORD your God with all your heart, with all your soul, and with all your strength. And these words which I command you today shall be in your heart. **You shall teach them diligently to your children**, and shall talk of them when you sit in your house, when you walk by the way, when you lie down, and when you rise up. You shall bind them as a sign on your hand, and they shall be as frontlets between your eyes. You shall write them on the door posts of your house and on your gates."*

Today, the door posts of our homes can be the Internet.

2

Cues From Nehemiah

The story of Nehemiah and his successful plan for rebuilding the broken walls of Jerusalem provides us with clear direction for restoring our families. With its broken walls, today's family, the basic unit of our society, has become unprotected and vulnerable. The enemy has had great success in breaking down our doors and sneaking in the windows through many of the entry-points already listed.

In Jerusalem, at the time of Nehemiah, it would seem the leaders and people living in the city had become reconciled to their sad state of affairs. They had resigned themselves to the confusion around them. Just as many people today live without hope of ever having happy, godly family relationships, the residents of Jerusalem lived in the rubble of their apathy. It took the deep caring and considered focus of one man—and obedience to His direction from God—to change the situation. Through his leadership, the Israelites regained hope, became willing to work together and enjoyed the reconstruction of what they had imagined to be forever ruined.

The biblical basis for making this analogy can be found in Romans 15:4.

"For everything that was written in the past was written to teach us, so that through the endurance taught in the Scriptures and the encouragement they provide we might have hope."

Within this context, the study of Nehemiah becomes amazingly relevant for the brokenness in our culture. The third chapter of Nehemiah lays out the plan the LORD gave Nehemiah for every family to take responsibility for the rubble of their environment. They were to rebuild the wall in consideration of those around them in order to reclaim the community, their city and their nation.

Preparation & Planning

Nehemiah didn't jump impulsively into the task. Before any of the work began—before he even made his intentions known—he went through a critical process of preparation. He cared about his people, sat down, mourned, fasted, prayed, repented, asked God to remember His promises and asked for favour. Those eight elements undergirded the project that lay before him. He didn't go through the entire process in an afternoon between lunch and dinner. He took *"some days."* He bared his heart to God and allowed Him to show him the depths of what had happened. It was a time of preparation for action, a time of becoming intimately attuned to the seriousness of the situation and what needed to be done.

Embarking upon this 52-day *Family Blessing Initiative* to build the prayer walls around your family and restore its strength is a mighty step. The preparation you make will set the tone for its effectiveness in your home. To assist you in this process, this chapter is formatted as a workbook, giving you opportunity to perform intentional preparation.

Why 52 Days?

When you think about it, 52 days is a strange number of days to take for the rebuilding of the wall of Jerusalem.

Josephus the historian records[7] the rebuilding of the wall, after the Jews returned from their captivity in Babylon, as taking place over a period of two years and four months. This extra time included the additional tasks such as further strengthening of various sections of the wall and embellishing and beautifying certain areas. The basic rebuilding, under the leadership of Nehemiah, however, took only 52 days, a momentous accomplishment that impressed even the enemies of Israel as a sign of the power of God. *"The wall was finished within 52 days. When all our enemies heard about it, and all the surrounding nations had seen it, they were deeply impressed and acknowledged that this work had been accomplished by the power of our God"*
(Nehemiah 6:15-16).

To understand God's ways and His Word, paying attention to the numbers found within its pages can be a remarkable aid. Dr. Ivan Panin, a Russian scientist and author of *Amazing New Discoveries*, was nominated for a Nobel prize for his work with the numeric aspects of the Hebrew and Greek alphabets. Their patterns in Scripture prove the Bible could not have been written by man, but only under the inspiration of a supernatural God. After his death, Panin's work was continued by Del Washburn and Alfred Nobel, and documented in a remarkable book, *Theomatics*.

The point is that nothing happens haphazardly or by chance with God. Every detail of His Word carries the

---

7.   Antiquities, 11.5.8

mark of divine design. Dr. Edward F. Vallowe, in his book *Biblical Mathematics* writes: "God has been called 'The Great Geometrician' and is said to do everything after a plan by number, weight and measure."[8]

So if nothing is haphazard with God, what significance does 52 days have? Why not 100 days—or 85 days?

This fifty-two days has great symbolic significance because it points directly to the wall of God that surrounds the heavenly Jerusalem (Zechariah 2:4-5). That wall, Scripture states, is a wall of fire in the midst of which is the grace and glory of God, His Holy Spirit, and it is imparted into us, forming a wall of grace around us and protecting us from Satan's power when we receive Him. .

The Holy Spirit appeared on earth at Pentecost, exactly 52 days after Jesus was crucified. The disciples were instructed to wait until the Holy Spirit came to them before they could begin to do the work of ministry. By sending the Holy Spirit on Pentecost, 52 days after the crucifixion, God confirmed that He had completed our wall of grace—the wall of the heavenly Jerusalem—because it was exactly the number of days that it took Nehemiah to complete the wall around the earthly Jerusalem when God's people returned from the first 'Babylon'.

As long as we walk within the grace-wall of the Holy Spirit, we will be protected during our journey on this earth. This grace-wall is everlasting and will keep us safe as long as we stay in God's Word.

And so the 52 days of our *Family Blessing Initiative* symbolizes a period of waiting on God to build the grace-walls of our family. Just as Nehemiah rebuilt the walls of unity and

8.   Vallow, Dr. Edward F., *Biblical Mathematics*, Olive Press (SC); Reprint edition July 1, 1997.

protection around Jerusalem, the Holy Spirit will help us to rebuild and restore the walls of our homes.

Here's what Nehemiah did:

1. *He had compassion for his people.* When Nehemiah heard from his brother about his people being in great trouble and disgrace, his heart went out to them. His sadness was evident to those around him. It was his deep compassion that motivated him to do something about the situation, to make a plan for the rebuilding of the broken walls. Compassion is an essential state of the heart for helping to heal broken, wounded people. When Jesus healed people, it was always His compassion that moved Him. The effect of much of the media today has been a general desensitization to the feelings and needs of those around us—particularly where it pertains to our families.

How I Feel About My Family (If your feelings are negative, ask God to give you His compassion —His heart for them.)

_____

_____

_____

2. *He sat down.* Amid all the frenetic activity and busyness, it's imperative that we stop, get a clear picture of the situation, evaluate the circumstances of our families and allow a reality check to come into clear focus. We have to take the bold step of eliminating the distractions that vie for our attention, whether social or technological, and dial in a clear picture of all the elements that constitute our families. Denial is rampant in the 21st

century. Allowing oneself to register a clear vision can be hugely challenging because it may mean confronting issues which could cause increased conflict. Sadly, denial leads only to delayed recognition, during which time enormous damage can be done. Only when we give God our full attention, can we hear His voice; only when we remove our hands from our eyes, can we see reality.

Taking Stock of My / Our Present Situation

3. *He mourned.* Mourning signifies a time of recognition of what has been lost. It is a grieving process. Finding oneself between what was (or what should have been) and the starkness of the present reality can be a very painful place. The weeping often associated with mourning can be a painful expression of grief. It can also serve as a gentle washing away of the past to make way for what is to come. Washing signifies cleansing or preparation to move ahead. We need hearts that can be so moved by the needs of our families that we are conduits of cleansing.

My Causes For Mourning

_____

_____

_____

_____

_____

_____

_____

_____

_____

_____

_____

_____

_____

_____

_____

4. *He fasted.* Fasting was a common practice during the exile but was certainly not confined to Old Testament practice. The Book of Acts gives us the example of believers fasting prior to making important decisions (Acts 13:4; 14:23). Fasting and prayer *together*—not just fasting and not just prayer—but both together at the same time, releases the flow of the Holy Spirit (Luke 2:37; 5:33-35). Too often, the focus of fasting is on the lack of food rather than on God, while the whole purpose must be to take our eyes off the things of this world and focus on Him. It's more than denying ourselves food or something else of the flesh; it's living a sacrificial lifestyle before God. Isaiah 58 says a *"true fast"* is not just an act of humility and denial before God but is a lifestyle of servant ministry to others. It encourages humility, loosens the chains of injustice, unties the chords of the yoke, frees the oppressed, feeds the hungry, provides for the poor, and clothes the naked. There's a promise of breakthrough that comes with, or after, fasting. *"Then your light shall break forth like the morning, your healing shall spring forth speedily, and your righteousness shall go before you; the glory of the LORD shall be your rear guard. Then you shall call, and the LORD will answer; you shall cry, and He will say, 'Here I am'"* (Isaiah 58:8-9).

But there's more!
"If you do away with the yoke of oppression, with the pointing finger and malicious talk, and if you spend yourselves in behalf of the hungry and satisfy the needs of the oppressed, then your light will rise in the darkness, and your night will become like the noonday."

How many of us, in our families, have pointed fingers in judgment, spoken behind each other's backs and piled oppressive fault and guilt on each other? That must be eliminated if we hope to see light rather than the darkness of despair.

"The LORD will guide you always; He will satisfy your needs in a sun-scorched land and will strengthen your frame. You will be like a well-watered garden, like a spring whose waters never fail. Your people will rebuild the ancient ruins and will raise up the age-old foundations; you will be called Repairer of Broken Walls, Restorer of Streets with Dwellings" (Isaiah 58:9b-12).

You will be called, *"Repairer of Broken Walls and Restorer of Streets with Dwellings!"* What are we doing other than trying to repair the broken walls and uneven streets of our family communities? This is a huge clue as to how we can be successful. We must look beyond our own needs to the needs of others.

So what does this mean for us in practical terms as preparation for the 52 days? That is entirely a personal decision. Ask God. Some may want to fast from food for a day or more, while others may feel led to be more helpful to others or live sacrificially in another way.

My Plan for Fasting

_____

_____

_____

_____

_____

He prayed. Nehemiah acknowledged God as the Supreme Source of Life, the Covenant Keeper, and asked Him to hear the prayer he was praying for his people. Nehemiah knew there was no point in trying to do anything of substance without an undergirding of prayer. James 5:16b (NIV) says, *"The prayer of a righteous person is powerful and effective."* The King James version is stronger. It says. *"The effectual fervent prayer of a righteous man availeth much* (emphasis added).*"*

When people pray fervently, God changes things. For us to hope our families will be restored without being willing to put the time in on our knees is a pipe dream. God works through our *prayers* - not our hopes.

When I (Diane) started this process of 52 days of prayer for my family, I found it very difficult to take the amount of time I felt was necessary to do the process justice. Of course I pray for my family all the time, but this was different. Nevertheless, I was trying to get this book written, edit another one, deal with a variety of issues and keep my business afloat, amongst other things. The LORD gave me a picture of myself, throwing little pebbles of prayer into the air expecting to build a wall of family restoration. I realized how ridiculous that would be and made prayer a priority in my life. The first night after doing that, a certain member of my family, who had de-friended me on Facebook about four months prior to this, suddenly, without stated reason, re-friended me. That was *huge* to me because I had felt so painfully excluded—and was now invited in again. A coincidence? I don't think so.

For anyone impatiently waiting to "feel" a connection to God or hear His voice, simply determining to speak in tongues for five or ten minutes can unlock the Spirit and prepare the way for "effectual, fervent prayer," where impatience is replaced by passion and a sense of disconnection is replaced by unquestioned connection.

Prayer is the umbilical cord tying us to God. We (like babies) are totally dependent on the life, power and spiritual nutrients that flow from the Father, through the cord of prayer, to us. Our need is connected to His supply through that cord. We have to ask—make our needs known—and then He sends what we need.

Why doesn't He just send the answer without us having to ask? That is the mystery of all creation. Why the all-sufficient God will do nothing in the lives of man without His requirement for prayer and intercession remains a mystery *until* one digs into His Word and discovers prayer is all about God training us to exercise the authority He has given us to implement His will on earth (Ezekiel 20:30-31). This earth is a boot camp—a place of preparation to fulfill the plans He has for us for eternity (1 Corinthians 6:2a,3a; 2 Timothy 2:12; Revelation 2:26; 5:9-10). By learning the ropes of spiritual warfare and how to connect with God through prayer, we learn how to become overcomers—how to enforce His will on earth. It's a high honour (Revelation 3:21) and it all happens through prayer and intercession.

Paul Bilheimer[9] said, "Heaven holds the key by which decisions governing earthly affairs are made, but we

---

9. Paul E. Bilheimer, *Destined for the Throne* (Fort Washington, Penn.: Christian Literature Crusade, Inc., 1978), p. 52.

hold the key by which those decisions are implement-
ed.... Prayer makes possible God's accomplishing what
He wants and what He cannot do without it."

In the process of developing *The Family Blessing Initiative,*
I (Val) have been battling cancer. I've been in and out of the
hospital on several occasions, but on November 15, 2012, I
had to have five litres of fluid drained from around my
collapsed left lung. The procedure itself was horrendous,
but out of it, the LORD showed me some spiritual applica-
tions for all of us who are praying for our families and others. Even when we don't think God is at work, He is.

I don't mean to gross you out with some of this. Hopefully
you will understand at the end.

As the surgeon went to work in my hospital room, Brenda
and all of our prayer team were praying. The room was
bathed in God's presence. The surgeon froze my left side,
but even with very large needles, was unable to access the
fluid. He finally gave up, having run into scar tissue that
was blocking the release of the fluid. He determined he
needed a new strategy. His plan was to map out a route
into the fluid with an ultrasound.

The next day, he arrived with a new plan. Again he froze
my left side. My lung had collapsed and had been lying
under five liters of fluid for many days. After some initial
probing, he said, "I'm into the fluid." They switched on
a three-liter vacuum container—but nothing happened.
When, at his command, I coughed, an obstruction suddenly
cleared. It was like a dam bursting. Three liters of fluid
gushed into the vacuum. My lung came free and ballooned
up. Air rushed in and it was so intense, it was like death
and life collided! Both arrived within me at the same in-

stant! Despite my desperate struggle to get air, I couldn't breath. They switched off the machine, but then all the nerve endings began to come to life in my lungs. I was sure I was going to die.

And then it happened. The breathing therapy nurse said "Breathe, Val, breath." I saw her hand reach for me, but then the veil of Heaven was opened and I saw all of these other hands pulling me up, up, up—away from death. But only the doctor and nurse were in my room.

A few minutes later, I was aware of the LORD showing me the power of prayer. The hands drawing me away from death had been the hands of people praying for me.

Several members of my prayer team had sent e-mails to me around the same time as the surgery procedure was happening. As I read them afterwards, I realized how God had shown me that our prayers travel into the fourth dimension (the spiritual realm). Dr. David Yongee Cho and Bill Johnston from Redding call it "Heaven touching Earth."

The LORD reminded me to tell all those who are praying for their families that *He is hearing all your prayers for your families! Amen....*

My Commitment to Pray for My Family

5. *He repented.* Nehemiah confessed not only the sins of his people but his own sins and those of his father's house, indicating the importance of addressing generational issues in repentance. The struggles we encounter in relationships are often rooted in generational sins that have never been broken off. Taking the time to ask God what these might be and drawing a blood line between us and those sins can be very important. If we truly want God to move us ahead in strengthening and healing individuals and relationships, we have to be sincere in turning away from attitudes, behaviors and actions that come between us and God. In short, we have to repent (be sorry for our sins and make the necessary changes).

Personal Repentance

_____

_____

_____

_____

_____

_____

_____

_____

_____

_____

_____

_____

_____

Standing in the Gap – Repenting for Generational Sins

Jeremiah 15:19 says, *"Therefore this is what the LORD says: 'If you repent, I will restore you that you may serve me; if you utter worthy, not worthless, words, you will be my spokesman. Let this people turn to you, but you must not turn to them.'"*

6. *He asked God to remember His promises.* If God has given you promises for your family through the years, this is a good time to remind Him of them.

Besides the promises God may have given you personally, Scripture is full of His promises to those who align themselves with His will (as revealed in His Word). Reminding Him of those promises by praying them back to Him opens heaven over your situation. Over the next 52 days, that is what we will be doing: praying God's Word back to Him on behalf of our families.

God's Promises Regarding my Family

_____

_____

_____

_____

_____

_____

_____

_____

_____

_____

_____

_____

_____

_____

_____

_____

7. *He asked for favor.* Nehemiah asked that God would give him success. In the same way, we can ask Him to give us success in the rebuilding of our families. It's important to note that the new wall Nehemiah built didn't look exactly like the old one. Some of the stones lying in the rubble of the old wall had changed shape in the process of tearing it down. Some were impossible to incorporate back into the wall. In rebuilding our families, we can't expect they will look exactly the way they used to look. Some of the pieces may have changed shape in the process of destruction. Some may be missing entirely. There may be new pieces that were not part of the original family. Changes in the components didn't prevent the rebuilding of a wonderful new wall around Jerusalem—and it needn't prevent the rebuilding of our families. Life goes on. Change is a part of growth.

My Prayer for God's Favour

_____

_____

_____

_____

_____

_____

_____

_____

_____

_____

_____

The Israelites rebuilt the wall around Jerusalem with build-ers tools in one hand and weapons in the other. The person chosen to blow the trumpet was to stay with Nehemiah so that he could signal to the people the areas where Nehemiah was directing them to work. For us, this means praying, hav-ing the Word of God sharply honed within us and staying tuned to the prompting of the Holy Spirit who will alert us to the areas where we need to build up the walls (strengthen our families). *"Our God will fight for us"* (Nehemiah 4:20). These words are for us today.

Jeremiah 23:29 says, *"'Is not My Word like fire,' declares the LORD, 'and like a hammer that breaks a rock in pieces?'"*

As we pray God's Word back to Him, it will be like a ham-mer, breaking the strongholds in our families.

The Israelites completed the task in 52 days because the people were committed to the task with all their hearts—as we must be if we are to see change in our families. Don't expect change with a half-hearted effort. God says when we seek Him *with all our hearts*, He will be found by us.

It was with this model, this *teaching from the past*, that the LORD gave us the call for 52 days of prayer—the *Family Blessing Initiative*. He said if families would commit them-selves to 52 days of prayer, He would bring restoration.

By rebuilding the walls of this generation, we are working to tighten and rebuild our relationships in our family, extend-ed family and community.

But in the rebuilding, we must never lose sight of who is actually accomplishing what needs to be done. Psalm 147:2-3 says, *"The LORD builds up Jerusalem; He gathers the exiles of Israel. He heals the brokenhearted and binds up their wounds."*

The Battle -
Taking the Step Beyond Diplomacy

As we seek to rebuild what has been destroyed, it is vital to understand that the family, the basic unit of society, has been under attack—and will continue to be attacked—by an enemy we can seldom see. This is no ordinary struggle.
We need help.

The *Family Blessing Initiative* takes the step beyond all the efforts to "fix" the family that haven't worked. We go beyond the counseling, beyond all the friendly advice from concerned co-workers, beyond all the self-help books, beyond all the seminars and yes, even beyond Dr. Phil's in-your-face insights. We take it to the next level, the supernatural level.

It's time to finally admit that many of our great philosophies regarding life aren't worth the time it took to dream them up. As knowledge has increased, our families have deteriorated.

Why? Because the human approach to problem solving can address only the physical, emotional and mental aspects of life. The brokenness in families and individuals today goes deeper than any of these. It's all about the spirit, the core of each individual. The only One who can heal a wounded spirit is the Holy Spirit.

The *Family Blessing Initiative* is a powerful, offensive strategy that invites supernatural intervention into our broken circumstances. We go to the top. We recognize that only God—the Creator of the universe—has the defining wisdom, the detailed understanding and the supernatural power to reach down into our struggles, pick us up individually, mend each wounded heart and knit us together into families that love each other.

When we enlist God to enter our circumstances and give Him the authority in our homes, we are not "trying" something new; we are *engaging Someone who is tried and true.* We are engaging the God who can send thousands of angels to fight on our behalf and rescue us. It's *amazing* how things change when we call on His Name and depend on Him.

We have an enemy (Satan) who has accomplished much destruction and will try to block the rebuilding. Ephesians 6:10-18 speaks of the importance of the armor of God and the wrestling we must expect on earth. It's a remarkable passage because it clarifies the nature of the enemy we have to fight and our responsibility in the battle.

Our homes have been invaded by the supernatural power of darkness. The only effective way to combat it is with the supernatural weapons God has given to us.

"Finally, be strong in the LORD and in His mighty power. Put on the full armor of God, so that you can take your stand against the devil's schemes. For our struggle is not against flesh and blood, but against the rulers, against the authorities, against the powers of this dark world and against the spiritual forces of evil in the heavenly realms. Therefore put on the full armor of God, so that when the day of evil comes, you may be able to stand your ground, and after you have done everything, to stand. Stand firm then, with the belt of truth buckled around your waist, with the breastplate of righteousness in place, and with your feet fitted with the readiness that comes from the gospel of peace. In addition to all this, take up the shield of faith, with which you can extinguish all the flaming ar-

rows of the evil one. Take the helmet of salvation and the sword of the Spirit, which is the word of God. And pray in the Spirit on all occasions with all kinds of prayers and requests. With this in mind, be alert and always keep on praying for all the LORD's people."

Having the Word of God sharply honed within us assures us of being properly equipped to be victorious over the battles that will challenge us.

Living Stones

The stones we use to rebuild our family walls are not hewn from impenetrable rock, but are "living stones."

1 Peter 2:4-7 says, *"As you come to Him, the living Stone—rejected by humans but chosen by God and precious to Him—you also, like living stones, are being built into a spiritual house to be a holy priesthood, offering spiritual sacrifices acceptable to God through Jesus Christ. For in Scripture it says: 'See, I lay a stone in Zion, a chosen and precious cornerstone, and the one who trusts in Him will never be put to shame.' Now to you who believe, this stone is precious. But to those who do not believe, 'The stone the builders rejected has become the cornerstone.'"*

That passage goes on to urge us to abstain from sinful desires that wage war against our souls. *"Live such good lives among the pagans that, though they accuse you of doing wrong, they may see your good deeds and glorify God on the day he visits us."*

The point is that as we pray, we are building grace-walls around our families from the "Living Stone"—Jesus Christ—and the good lives we lead as "living stones" will serve as evidence that God is real and is truly living within us.

Overcoming the "Four Ds" – Discouragement, Disappointment, Despair and Depression

Being prepared for the opposition that is sure to come (often in the form of the "Four Ds" - discouragement, disappointment, despair and depression) is critical.

When Nehemiah and the people of Jerusalem had the wall built to half its height, opposition from their enemies, Sanballat and Tobias, intensified (Nehemiah 4). Having been vocal in their ridicule at the beginning, when the success of the rebuilding began to become evident, the two became very angry, made threats and did all they could to intimidate the Israelites into stopping the work.

Like Nehemiah, we must be prepared for opposition in our efforts to rebuild. There will always be those who oppose and ridicule us, even in our own households—sometimes particularly in our own households.

It may appear that opposition comes from resistant family members, but the real source of the opposition comes from Satan. While it's true that aspects of humanity cannot be overlooked as culprits, Satan can be found at the root. Things make more sense when we remember that the issue that messed him up in the first place was his jealousy of God. He wanted to destroy whatever God was doing. That has not changed. His attacks are designed to intimidate, cause fear and destroy the godly unity and strength of our families.

Nehemiah calmed the fears of the nobles and the families by saying, *"Don't be afraid of them. Remember the LORD, who is great and awesome—and fight for your families, your sons and your daughters, your wives and your homes"* (Nehemiah 4:14-15). *"When our enemies heard that we were aware of their plot and that God had frustrated it, we all returned to the wall, each to our own work...Our God will fight for us"* (Nehemiah 4:20).

Again, like Nehemiah, we must keep our eyes fixed on the work we are doing, knowing God is at work on our behalf. Our part is to take the responsibility of leadership in our homes, do the work of praying diligently and leave the outcome to Him.

The people of Jerusalem were clear about the need for having swords in their hands while they rebuilt. Like them, we must continue to be clear about our need for spiritual weapons as we do the work of rebuilding. While carrying a physical sword might seem like more tangible evidence of warfare, the spiritual weapons of our warfare are no less—in fact, are more—powerful; but they need to be *used* to be of any benefit.

Jeremiah 23:29 says, *"'Is not my Word like fire,' declares the LORD, 'and like a hammer that breaks a rock in pieces?'"* When we get truly in the presence of God, and receive His Word concerning some of the rubble and huge issues standing in the way of our family restoration, we can be assured that the rubble can be burned away and the issues can be broken down into bits we can easily handle.

Praise is an invaluable weapon for routing the enemy and overcoming the Four Ds. Psalm 149:5-6 says, *"Let the saints be joyful in glory: let them sing aloud upon their beds. Let the high praises of God be in their mouth, and a two-edged sword in their hand..."* For that reason, we have included the vital component of praise in the 52 days of prayer.

Isaiah 61:3 says the LORD gives us *"the oil of joy instead of mourning, and a garment of praise instead of a spirit of despair."*

The Four Ds will disappear as we truly enter into praise.

Praise is the greatest weapon against anything we can ever face. It is our greatest, greatest weapon. Praise releases into the atmosphere the LORDship and the greatness and the majesty of God. If there is anything the enemy hates, it's us praising and worshipping our LORD.

There are countless testimonies of how lives and families have been changed through relentless praise—people who have demonstrated their trust in God by giving Him steadfast praise throughout the difficulties of life.

I (Diane) can testify to the importance of praise in routing the Four Ds. When my home was shattered six years ago through traumatic events, my grief was so deep that sometimes when I wept, it was like primal groans rising to my lips from eons of antiquity, carrying with them the pain of humanity wounded by sin from the dawn of time. I had no words. Transitioning that pain into a sacrifice of praise to God was literally my key to survival (Psalm 54:6; Hebrews 13:15).

In the process of developing the *Family Blessing Initiative*, Val and Brenda have been undergoing one of the greatest challenges of their lives, battling Val's cancer. I called tonight to find out how he was. He had just returned from the hospital after having a liter of fluid drained from his lung—and still, he and Brenda were giving praise to God for His awesome goodness. Amazing!

If it seems that taking time to praise is slowing you down in getting to the "real business" of praying for your family, you're missing its unmatched value. You're missing the path to the heart of God. You're missing His dwelling-place. God dwells in the praise of His people.

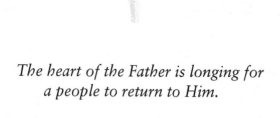

The heart of the Father is longing for
a people to return to Him.

3

Taking Up Our Positions

The trumpet is blowing, signaling someone in the home to rise up in leadership to lead your family into restoration.

Leadership in many homes today needs to be restored. It has become commonplace to find parents more intent on popularity with their families than on guiding them to successful, godly lives.

"I looked for a man among them who would build up the wall and stand before Me in the gap on behalf of the land, so I would not have to destroy it, but I found none" (Ezekiel 22:30).

Reeling from the ridicule reflected on them from television sitcoms, feminist agendas and backlashed efforts to find their footing as men, many men fear appearing to take any kind of leadership role in their homes. They fear being labeled as "authoritarian," "aggressive" or "controlling."

In a similar manner, many women who might normally excel in the leadership role are so stressed from over-commitment, overwork and societal confusion, that it's easier to let things slide than address the issues required to set their homes in order. In the vacuum of leadership, the demands of disconnected children often own the stage.

Through the *Family Blessing Initiative*, families are being called to recognize the critical function of leaders in the home and support them in presiding over the family altar.

While it is usual to have one person who takes this position, where families commit to rebuilding together, it may work to share the leadership role in whatever way works for your family. The important thing is to establish leadership, commit to the 52 days of prayer for your family, begin and be faithful.

The Table Today - Oak or Cyber?

In days gone by, the father of the home would assemble the family around the family table, but things have changed.

The table today is not always the solid oak structure, the central piece of furniture in the home. Sometimes the gathering place today is in cyberspace via a private family Facebook page. Sometimes it's a prearranged Skype call or conference call. Sometimes it's a group e-mail.

Wherever possible, the tangible oak table is still the optimal place for a family to meet to share a meal, share hopes, laughter, concerns and prayer. There's nothing like holding the hands of loved ones in a prayer circle around a family table.

But 21st Century living has changed and we must find ways to adapt and work with new ways of doing things. Where families are unable to meet face to face, the same technology that has served to isolate individuals can be redeemed to restore family bonds.

What is Your Position?

In rebuilding the Jerusalem wall, Nehemiah was very detailed in appointing particular people with particular giftings to particular areas of the wall.

For the purposes of the *Family Blessing Initiative,* we have identified three divisions of builders, all representing various aspects of the home. Sometimes these may overlap (i.e. computer-savvy grandparents can also provide cyber security).

HOMELAND SECURITY—Parents and guardians

LEGACY SECURITY—Grandparents

CYBER SECURITY—Computer savvy, empty-nesters

It's interesting to note that, while the importance of the Church (the assembly of believers) is emphasized throughout Scripture, it is never earmarked as the primary teacher of faith to children and grandchildren. Parents (guardians) and grandparents are responsible for the spiritual education of the home (i.e. 2 Timothy 1:5).

Homeland Security

Parents (whether single or not) living at home with their children are encouraged to gather the family around the table daily. This is a wonderful opportunity to train children in living lives of gratitude and prayer. The example parents set of practising a solid relationship with God and acknowledging Him as the foundation of the home is priceless in establishing genuine security for a child. Security in God transcends the ups and downs of all earthly circumstances.

If children complain about devotions being "boring," they're not alone. Depending on the home and the approach to prayer time, they may be quite justified in their complaints. The thing is parents are going to vary in their ability to present prayer and the Word of God in a compelling way, but as long as it is presented lovingly, eventually there will be fruit. God's Word never returns to Him void, meaning something will have been accomplished by it being spoken or read. Whether or not a time of devotions have been part of a home, it is never too late to begin.

Faithfulness always trumps boredom. Boredom is not justification for discontinuing something valuable; it may be simply a signal that something needs to be tweaked.

Legacy Security

Countless stories echo through the ages of the prayers and godly examples of grandparents whose undergirding of faith made the difference in the lives of their families.

Grandparenting in the 21st Century differs radically from that of previous generations. Many grandparents today feel shell-shocked by the fallout from divorces in the lives of family around them. Some find themselves shut out of the lives of their loved ones, while others struggle to raise their children's children. Their hearts ache for the young ones, many of whom are shifted from home to home as parents try to cope with the massive complications accompanying divorce, remarriage and single parenting.

Many lie awake at night, fretting about how different life could be if only their families would recognize and reject the ungodly influences that converge to destroy them. In seeking to immobilize them with worry, Satan attempts to destroy the grandparents as well as the children. After tossing and turning night after night, sometimes feeling at the mercy of tormenting spirits trying to eat my brain, I (Diane) found the only way for me to overcome their efforts was to say the Name of Jesus— over and over and over again, until sleep finally came. As long as I filled my mind with His Name, there was no space for torment. We must stay strong for our families, but the only way to do that is through the Spirit of God.

For many young people, the homes of their grandparents represent the only stability they know in a world rocked by instability. Without a clear understanding and demonstration of the heritage of faith and godly values that hopefully serves as their foundation, they may be at the mercy of a secularist society that loudly proclaims its ungodly values.

The *Family Blessing Initiative* is a clarion call to grandparents to pray and stand fast for the strengthening and restoration of their families. We must carry the baton of godly stability across uncharted terrain.

Cyber Security

Empty-nesters whose circumstances prevent physical gathering of the family can take advantage of technology to participate in the *Family Blessing Initiative* in non-traditional ways (i.e.: by forming a family Facebook group in which they post daily for 52 days). Thanks to social media, it's now possible to commit to daily spiritual leadership in cyberspace.

Setting up a private family Facebook page, where members stop by daily to see who has posted what about their day, can be a great point of contact, one that can be particularly meaningful to those missing the sounds and smells and familiar faces of home. I (Diane), in testing the plan, became very discouraged at one point because my family was not responding in the way I had hoped. So I posted an e-mail, saying I was no longer going to clog up their inboxes with something they did not appear to value. My granddaughter wrote back with this note: "No Grandma, please don't stop. Just because I haven't responded doesn't mean I don't like it. I read it every night and it makes me feel as though our family is connected." Needless to say, I never missed a night after that.

The priest of the home (leader) takes the responsibility of posting a passage of scripture and a prayer of blessing. He or she may also take the opportunity of making a proclamation or declaration of God's will, according to His Word, over the family.

Where a family gathers through conference calling or Skyping, the leader simply records pertinent comments in this workbook and uses the scripture and prayer guides as he or she would if all were gathered around the family oak table.

During the 52-day *Family Blessing Initiative*, the scriptural promises, prayers for family blessing and proclamations over the family can be copied directly into daily Facebook or e-mail posts. The "Answers, Changes and Thoughts" become "comments" under the posts.

Daily Strategy—the "Four P's" Plan

- Praise
- Promise, Proverb or Precept
- Prayer for God's Blessing on Our Family

- Proclamation/Declaration of God's Grace Over Our Family
  Job 22:27-28 reads *"You will also declare a thing, and it will be established for you; so light will shine on your ways."* Obviously, the words we write or speak can be tools God uses to change our circumstances—when infused with faith. Making proclamations or declarations over our circumstances may not be something many of us remember our parents doing over us, but its importance is becoming increasingly recognized as scriptural directives are being increasingly revealed to us.

Praying God's Promises Back to Him

The practice of praying God's promises back to Him is powerful. God created the heavens and the earth by speaking them into existence. By praying His promises back to Him, we are speaking God's will for our lives into being. He promises His Word will not return to Him void. Isaiah 55:11 (NKJV) reads, *"So shall My Word be that goes forth from My mouth; it shall not return to Me void, but it shall accomplish what I please, and it shall prosper in the thing for which I sent it.* When we speak God's words back to Him as prayer, they return to Him full of our desire for their fulfillment and expectation of His faithfulness.

For that reason, the 52 days of prayer in the *Family Blessing Initiative* are all built on praying God's promises and proverbs back to Him.

God told Joshua that if he wanted to be successful, he needed to meditate on God's Word both day and night and to keep it always on his lips (Joshua 1:8).

"By wisdom a house is built, and by understanding it is established; and by knowledge the rooms are filled with all precious and pleasant riches." Proverbs 24: 3-4

"He then brought them out and asked, 'Sirs what must I do to be saved?' They replied, 'Believe in the LORD Jesus, and you will be saved—you and your household.'" Acts 16:30-31

My / Our Greatest Hopes
for the Next 52 Days

The army of God
must get back all that has been stolen.
The battle is fought on our knees.

*"For this reason I kneel before the Father, from Whom every
family in heaven and on earth derives its name."*
Ephesians 3:14-15

5

Ready to Begin

When an author writes a book, he or she generally closes with the key to the entire book. The hope is that the last thing written will be remembered by the reader. Malachi is the last book of the Old Testament. It contains the essence of God's message to us. Not surprisingly, it's all about relationship to Him and to our families.

Malachi 4:5-6 reads, *"See, I will send you the prophet Elijah before that great and dreadful day of the LORD comes. He will turn the hearts of the fathers to their children, and the hearts of the children to their fathers; or else I will come and strike the land with a curse."*

In the New Testament, Jesus said (of John), *"And he will go on before the LORD, in the spirit and power of Elijah, to turn the hearts of the fathers to their children and the disobedient to the wisdom of the righteous—to make ready a people prepared for the LORD"* (Luke 1:17).

Who are these people who are being made ready and "prepared for the LORD"? You and me! Jesus said to His disciples,

"But the Counselor, (the Comforter, Consoler, Paraclete) *the Holy Spirit whom the Father will send in My Name, will*

instruct you in everything, and remind you of all that I have done. 'Peace' is My farewell to you, My peace is My gift to you" (John 14:26-27).

A Prayer to Begin the 52-Day Journey

Father, we are ready to begin this 52-day journey of restoration with You. We give you all our hopes, dreams and failed attempts to make our home what we know it should be.

Father, we lay down all those tools of darkness that have caused confusion and brokenness in our family. We reject the ways of our enemy, Satan. We ask you to forgive our selfishness, our unkind attitudes, our rebellion against Your ways and our lack of trust in You. We're asking for a second chance for our family, a new day where we can start fresh. Please strengthen and enlarge our faith and trust in You.

Father, we know that the behaviors that have caused the difficulties in our relationships have become deeply ingrained. We ask for Your supernatural intervention to set us free from them and renew our minds into healthy conformity with You.

We invite You into our lives to make our home a joyful sanctuary where You are central and we live lives that are truly pleasing to You. We know when we do things Your way, we will be able to walk into the wonderful destiny you have planned and prepared for us.

In the name of Jesus. Amen.

Day One

Praise: Holy Spirit, You are welcome in our home. I/we invite You into our home and family. We look to You as our Helper, our Counselor, our Comforter, our Teacher, our Healer and our Deliverer. Father God, we give You praise as the Most High God. We want to bless You and please You, because You are worthy of all glory honour and praise.

Promise: "I am the LORD that healeth thee" Exodus 15:26.

Prayer & Blessing for Our Family:

Father God, thank You for our family. We come before You on this first day with renewed hope that we can live in the light and joy of Your blessing. We're asking You to help us to clear the rubble from our lives so that we can live in the blessing You purposed for us. We come to You, asking You to heal us in every way: in our body, soul, spirit and relationships. Thank You, LORD. In Jesus' name we pray. Amen.

Proclamation Over Our Family:

In the name of Jesus Christ of Nazareth, I speak healing over my family and thank You, O LORD, for Your goodness and grace.

Requests

_____

_____

_____

_____

_____

Answers, Changes & Thoughts

Day Two

Praise: Father God, You are Holy. There is no god that can compare to You. You reign supreme and we worship You.

Precept: Psalm 16:8 says, "I have set the LORD always before me: because He is at my right hand, I shall not be moved."

Prayer & Blessing for Our Family:

Father God, thank You for Your faithfulness and for protecting each of us where we are. I know that if we are mindful of You going before us and we honour You with our thoughts and plans, we'll be okay and we'll be able to fulfill your plans for our lives. Throughout these difficult years, You have always been at my right hand and so I shall not be moved. I shall continue to trust You for myself and on behalf of my dear family. Amen.

Proclamation Over Our Family:

In the Name of the Messiah, Jesus Christ of Nazareth, I proclaim the God of Abraham, Isaac and Jacob to be LORD over my family.

Requests

_____

_____

_____

_____

_____

_____

_____

Answers, Changes & Thoughts

Day Three

Praise: Father God, we give glory and praise to You, for you are gracious and compassionate and we worship You.

Promise: 2 Chronicles 30:9 says, "For if you turn again unto the LORD, your brothers (and sisters) and your children shall find compassion before them that lead them captive ... for the LORD your God is gracious and merciful, and will not turn away His face from you, if you return unto Him."

Prayer & Blessing for Our Family:

Father God, thank You for this day. I pray Your blessing on every household represented in this family. I pray You will give each one health, wisdom, clarity of mind, hearts to honour You, prosperity, satisfying relationships and the ability to affect our culture in a positive way. Thank You for Your promise that, as I keep my eyes fixed on You, my brothers and sisters and children (and grandchildren) will receive favour in this life. Thank You for Your grace and mercy towards us and Your promise not to turn Your face away from us as we turn to You. In Jesus' Name we pray. Amen.

Proclamation Over Our Family:

In the Name of Jesus Christ of Nazareth, I speak restoration over my family.

Requests

_____
_____
_____
_____
_____
_____
_____
_____

Answers, Changes & Thoughts

_____
_____
_____
_____
_____
_____
_____
_____
_____
_____
_____
_____
_____
_____

Day Four

Praise: Father God, we praise You as the God of all wisdom, understanding and grace. We love You, LORD.

Proverb: Proverbs 24:3-4 says, "By wisdom a house is built, and by understanding it is established; and by knowledge, the rooms are filled with all precious and pleasant riches"

Prayer & Blessing for Our Family:

Father God, I bring my family before You this day and ask for Your great wisdom. I know that the "fear of the LORD" is the beginning of wisdom, and that is what we need. We need your knowledge and understanding so that our relationships will be filled with all of Your pleasant blessings and riches. I pray this home will be built and established with your wisdom. Today I am asking, as James 1:5 instructs, "Ask God for wisdom and He will give generously to all." It was also said of Jesus that He "kept increasing in wisdom" (Luke 2:52). That is what we need Father: to keep increasing in Your wisdom. Amen.

Proclamation Over Our Family:

In the Name of Jesus Christ of Nazareth, I speak the mind of Christ over my family, filling each of us with Your wisdom, knowledge and understanding. Thank You, LORD.

_____

_____

_____

_____

_____

Requests

Answers, Changes & Thoughts

Day Five

Praise: Father God, You know all things and do all things well. We bring praise and adoration to You LORD.

Promise: Jeremiah 29:11-13 says, 'I know the plans I have for you,' declares the LORD, 'plans to prosper you and not to harm you, plans to give you hope and a future. Then you will call on Me and come and pray to Me, and I will listen to you. You will seek Me and find Me when you seek Me with all your heart.'

Prayer & Blessing for Our Family:

Father God, please move among us and stir us to seek You with all our hearts. Help us to really know You and find how to live the abundant life You came to give us. Please reveal Your plans for us as we seek You. Strengthen and equip us to fulfill them. We give You all the disappointments we have experienced and ask You to turn them around for our good. Please heal those in pain and give us hearts of gratitude. Thank You, Father, for Your love. In Jesus' name. Amen.

Proclamation Over Our Family:

In the Name of Jesus Christ of Nazareth, I speak healing over our family. I declare that, through the knowledge of Christ, we will enjoy discovering God's plan for each of our lives and fulfill our purpose on earth.

Requests

_____
_____
_____
_____
_____
_____
_____
_____

Answers, Changes & Thoughts

_____
_____
_____
_____
_____
_____
_____
_____
_____
_____
_____
_____
_____

Day Six

Praise: Father God, we praise and honour You for who You are and what You are doing in our lives. You are our wonderful Counselor, God of all mercy and grace.

Promise: Luke 15:20 says, "So he got up and went to his father. But while he was still a long way off, his father saw him and was filled with compassion for him; he ran to his son, threw his arms around him and kissed him."

Prayer & Blessing for Our Family:

Father God, You always welcome us home. You do not condone our sins nor do You condemn us, but You forgive us when we express regret and determine to make changes. We see what kind of love You have for us. You call us "son" and "daughter." Thank You that You never change. Please bless and protect each dear one. In the name of Jesus we pray. Amen.

Proclamation Over Our Family:

In the name of Jesus Christ of Nazareth, I speak breakthrough over our family, that God will answer our prayers swiftly and that all obstacles to our family unity will be removed.

Requests

_____

_____

_____

_____

Answers, Changes & Thoughts

Day Seven

Praise: Father God, we praise You as the Creator of our world and all the worlds beyond.

Promise: Job 22 27-28 says, "You will make your prayer to Him, He will hear you, and you will pay your vows. You will also declare a thing, and it will be established for you; so light will shine on your ways."

Prayer & Blessing for Our Family:

Father God, thank You for hearing our prayers. It is amazing that You have given us the ability to speak (declare) Your will into being on earth. Thank You for infusing our words with Your supernatural power to change our circumstances. Please fill our words with Your blessing over us.

Proclamation Over Our Family:

In the name of Jesus Christ of Nazareth, I declare, in accord with the will of heaven, that unity and love will be restored in my house.

Requests

_____

_____

_____

_____

_____

_____

Answers, Changes & Thoughts

Day Eight

Praise: Father God, we honour You and thank You for Your Word, so filled with healing and blessing and love.

Proverb: Proverbs 12:18 says, "Reckless words pierce like a sword, but the tongue of the wise brings healing."

Prayer & Blessing for Our Family:

Father God, we desire to bless and affirm each other in the name of Jesus. We break off any generational "reckless" words or curses spoken over us from the past. In the same manner, we call forth all of the stolen blessings that our family has missed. In Jesus' name and by His precious blood. Amen.

Proclamation Over Our Family:

In the name of Jesus Christ of Nazareth, we speak freedom from the effects of reckless words spoken over us, either generationally or directly and decree that the devourer will no longer consume the blessings of our family.

Requests

_____

_____

_____

_____

_____

_____

Answers, Changes & Thoughts

Day Nine

Praise: Father God, we praise You as the Source of all wisdom, knowledge and direction. We love You, LORD.

Promise: Psalm 32:8 says, "I will instruct you and teach you in the way which you shall go: I will guide you with My eye."

Prayer & Blessing for Our Family:

Father God, thank You for not leaving us alone to struggle blindly through life. Thank You for assuring us that You will instruct us if we really listen for Your voice and seek You with all our hearts. Thank You for Your promise to guide us. I pray Your blessing on every one of my family and pray that You will heal anything in their bodies or minds that needs healing. Please help them with any troubling circumstances. In Jesus' name I pray. Amen.

Proclamation Over Our Family:

In the name of Jesus Christ of Nazareth, I speak blessing and the direction of the LORD over my family.

Requests

Answers, Changes & Thoughts

Day Ten

Praise: Father God, we honour You as the Source of all truth. You are the Way, the Truth and the Life. No one can connect with God except through You.

Promise: 3 John 4 says, "I have no greater joy than to hear that my children are walking in the truth."

Prayer & Blessing for Our Family:

Heavenly Father, we are grateful for Your truth. There are so many philosophies and beliefs vying for our acceptance these days that it can get very confusing, particularly for young people who are trying to find their way. I pray You will bless us with hearts and minds open and attuned to the truth of the Most High God and protect us from falling for anything less. Thank you for Your love and care for each of us. In Jesus' name I pray. Amen.

Proclamation Over Our Family:

In the name of Jesus Christ of Nazareth, I declare that every weapon the enemy tries to use against us will be given over into our hands and used against him for his destruction—with powerful breakthroughs for God. I render every false philosophy that seeks to destroy our faith, impotent.

Requests

_____

_____

_____

_____

Answers, Changes & Thoughts

Day Eleven

Praise: Father God, we give You praise for who You are. You are our Rock, our High Tower, our very present help in time of trouble. We love You, LORD.

Promise: Hebrews 11:6 says, "Without faith it is impossible to please God, because anyone who comes to Him must believe that He exists and that He rewards those who earnestly seek Him."

Prayer & Blessing for Our Family:

Heavenly Father, we're grateful for the day. Thank you for the strength, health, motivation, resources, opportunities and abilities to do all we've accomplished today. There's nothing greater that we could ask than to please You. You hold our future in Your hands. You say we please You with our faith —and so, LORD, we ask for an increase in our faith. We ask that You would reveal Yourself more clearly to each one of us and help us to believe more completely. Please open our eyes to all the evidences of Your existence You've given in nature. Help us to really "get it." Thank You from the bottom of our hearts for all the rewards You have given us for seeking You earnestly. In Jesus' name we pray. Amen.

Proclamation Over Our Family:

In the name of Jesus Christ of Nazareth, I speak an increase in faith over my family.

Requests

_____
_____
_____
_____
_____
_____
_____

Answers, Changes & Thoughts

_____
_____
_____
_____
_____
_____
_____
_____
_____
_____
_____
_____
_____

Day Twelve

Praise: We bless You, LORD, and magnify Your holy Name. Sweet Holy Spirit, we adore You and offer You all our praise.

Promise: Hebrews 1:14 says, "Are they (angels) not all ministering spirits, sent forth to minister for them who shall be heirs of Salvation?"

Prayer & Blessing for Our Family:

Father, we thank You for the angels You send to help us in times of need. Thank You, that when we can't be with our loved ones in times of trauma or stress, we can ask You to send Your angels to minister to them and know they're being looked after. And when dear ones seem so far away, we can ask You to help them feel Your presence so they aren't alone. I pray You will bless each home represented by our family and keep everyone safe. In Jesus' name. Amen.

Proclamation Over Our Family:

In the name of Jesus Christ of Nazareth, I declare the peace of God and His blessing.

Requests

_____

_____

_____

_____

_____

_____

_____

Answers, Changes & Thoughts

Day Thirteen

Praise: Father God, we worship You. We worship You.

Promise: Psalm 23 says, "He makes me to lie down in green pastures: He leads me beside the still waters. He restores my soul: He leads me in the paths of righteousness for His Name's sake. Though I walk through the valley of the shadow of death, I will fear no evil: for You are with me; Your rod and Your staff they comfort me."

Prayer & Blessing for Our Family:

Father, thank You for giving us a safe place to sleep and live. Thank You for leading us in paths of peace and restoration. Because of the faithfulness we have found in You, we know we do not need to fear any evil. You are with us and will protect us as we keep our eyes steadily on You. You are our place of safety, comfort and restoration, the place where we get replenished and find resources to share with others. Thank You for all the comfort You have given us over the years. You are our rock, a sure place to stand. Though the mountains may be shaken, we are safe in You, no matter where we are. LORD, please bless our family tonight. Help them feel Your arms lovingly around them. In Jesus' name. Amen.

Proclamation Over Our Family:

In the name of Jesus Christ of Nazareth, I speak restoration, righteousness and the comfort of the LORD over my family.

_____

_____

_____

Requests

_____
_____
_____
_____
_____
_____
_____

Answers, Changes & Thoughts

_____
_____
_____
_____
_____
_____
_____
_____
_____
_____
_____
_____
_____

Day Fourteen

Praise: Father God, to You we lift our hearts in praise and gratitude. Your love and kindness is endless towards us.

Promise: 1 Peter 3: 8,9 really illustrates the nature of blessing. "Finally, all of you should live together in peace. Try to understand each other. Love each other as brothers. Be kind and humble. Do not do wrong to a person to pay him back for doing wrong to you. Or do not insult someone to pay him back for insulting you. But ask God to bless that person. Do this, because you yourselves were called to receive a blessing."

Prayer & Blessing for Our Family:

Dear LORD, we are grateful that You are a God of peace and You teach us how to live in peace with one another. Please help us to understand each other more fully and more deeply and have compassion for the areas of imperfection we all have. Please give us patience and love for each other as we work through those areas. Please guard our hearts from judgements and ungodly agendas. I pray You will bless our family tonight, LORD. Keep everyone safe, healthy and encouraged. Please heal any physical ailments and any difficult emotional issues among us. In Jesus' name we pray. Amen.

Proclamation Over Our Family:

In the Name of Jesus Christ of Nazareth, I declare the blessing of the LORD over my family.

_____

_____

_____

Requests

_____

Answers, Changes & Thoughts

_____

Day Fifteen

Praise: Father God, With our lips we give You praise. With our hearts we honour You. With our lives we long to bless You.

Promise: Psalm 115:12-15 says, "The LORD remembers us and will bless us...He will bless those who fear the LORD—small and great alike. May the LORD make you increase, both you and your children. May you be blessed by the LORD, the Maker of heaven and earth."

Prayer & Blessing for Our Family:

Father, we thank You for Your personal, individual care for each one of us. It's amazing tho think that You "remember" us. When I look out of an airplane and see how incredibly small man is and how many of us there are, it's amazing to think You are mindful of each of us individually and that You created everything we see. You have told us that the fear of the LORD is the beginning of wisdom—and so I pray for wisdom for my family so You will be able to bless each of their precious lives. In Jesus' name. Amen.

Proclamation Over Our Family:

In the name of Jesus Christ of Nazareth, I declare increase and blessing over my family in whatever way it is needed. Thank You, LORD.

Requests

_____
_____
_____
_____
_____
_____
_____
_____

Answers, Changes & Thoughts

_____
_____
_____
_____
_____
_____
_____
_____
_____
_____
_____
_____
_____
_____

Day Sixteen

Praise: Father God, we will bless You at all times. Your praise will be continually in our mouths.

Proverb: Proverbs 14:26 says, "He who fears the LORD has a secure fortress, and for his children it will be a refuge."

Prayer & Blessing for Our Family:

Dear LORD, You know how we try to really pay attention to Your Word because we know it's true. We're grateful that You reward that respect with security in You. We're so thankful that You are faithful to Your Word. I pray that my children and grandchildren will always know they have a refuge in You. I pray You will bless, guide and protect each precious one and teach them Your ways. In Jesus' name. Amen.

Proclamation Over Our Family:

In the name of Jesus Christ of Nazareth, I speak breakthrough in all aspects of my family and reject all obstacles that would seek to hinder the breakthrough of the Holy Spirit in our lives.

Requests

_____

_____

_____

_____

_____

_____

_____

Answers, Changes & Thoughts

Day Seventeen

Praise: Father God, we worship You in Spirit and in truth from our hearts and minds and souls. We lift our praise and adoration to You, the Light of our lives.

Promise: Deuteronomy 4:40 says, "Keep His decrees and commands, which I am giving you today, so that it may go well with you and your children after you and that you may live long in the land the LORD your God gives you for all time."

Prayer & Blessing for Our Family:

Dear LORD, Sometimes we feel totally inadequate to measure up to Your standards. Thank You for Your mercy and grace and the way You teach us so patiently. Thank You for giving us Your Holy Spirit to live through our lives. Please strengthen us to walk in Your will because when we do things Your way, things work out so much better. In Jesus' name. Amen.

Proclamation Over Our Family:

In the name of Jesus, I speak the righteousness of Christ over every member of my family. You promised, LORD, that Your Word would not return to You void, so I speak fullness and life into every scripture they have ever read, heard or spoken in their whole lives and pray it would bear fruit. I declare them free of all generational hindrances that would keep them from walking in the faith and fullness of Your Holy Spirit. I speak the blessing of the LORD over them and, through the authority given to me in Christ Jesus, I break off all the effects of trauma, shock or disappointment in their lives so they can walk in liberty, freedom, strength and happiness. I speak Your wisdom and success over them.

Requests

_____
_____
_____
_____
_____
_____
_____

Answers, Changes & Thoughts

_____
_____
_____
_____
_____
_____
_____
_____
_____
_____
_____
_____
_____
_____
_____

Day Eighteen

Praise: Father God, with humble hearts and in sincere devotion, we give You praise. You are our source and our help in time of trouble.

Promise: John 14:25 says, "The Counselor, the Holy Spirit, whom the Father will send in My Name, will teach you all things and will remind you of everything I have said to you. Peace I leave with you, My peace I give you. I do not give to you as the world gives. Do not let your hearts be troubled and do not be afraid."

Prayer & Blessing for Our Family:

Dear LORD, Thank You for Your Holy Spirit. LORD, I pray that You will bless my family with the full knowledge of who You are, that they would not just know You in their heads but that You would supernaturally fill each one full to overflowing with Your Holy Spirit. Fill them with Your joy and power and peace, LORD. Help them to live life fully in You so their lives will be full of the peace that only You can give. I pray that no matter what fears this world may bring them, they will be able to relax in the knowledge that they are not alone but that You love them and will care about every detail as they look to You. In Jesus' name I pray. Amen.

Proclamation Over Our Family:

In the name of Jesus, I speak the love, peace and power of the Holy Spirit over my family. I speak safety and wisdom over each precious one.

Requests

Answers, Changes & Thoughts

Day Nineteen

Praise: Father God, You are the Light of our lives. We praise and bless You, LORD, the Source of all Light.

Promise: Ephesians 5:8 says "For you were once darkness, but now you are light in the LORD: walk as children of light (for the fruit of the light consists in all goodness righteousness and truth) and find out what pleases the LORD."

Prayer & Blessing for Our Family:

Dear LORD, Thank You that when we open our lives up to You, You remove the darkness by filling us with Your light. I pray that Your Holy Spirit will draw every member of our family to experience the light of Your love. I pray You will give each one an insatiable appetite for your Word because it's only in You, our Creator, that we can really find our true purpose. Only Your presence can fill up all the corners with fulfillment and deep peace. Help us, LORD, to walk as children of light. In Jesus' name. Amen.

Proclamation Over Our Family:

In the name of Jesus, I speak light and goodness and righteousness over my family.

Requests

_____
_____
_____
_____
_____
_____
_____
_____

Answers, Changes & Thoughts

_____
_____
_____
_____
_____
_____
_____
_____
_____
_____
_____
_____
_____

Day Twenty

Praise: Father God, we rest in You. You are our hiding place, a safe place during any storm. All our praise is due You.

Precept: Deuteronomy 6:6,7 says, "These commandments that I give you today are to be upon your hearts. Impress them on your children. Talk about them when you sit at home and when you walk along the road, when you lie down and when you get up."

Prayer & Blessing for Our Family:

Dear LORD, I am thankful that no matter what may come or go in our lives, You are faithful and Your Word is the rock upon which we stand. Though the earth may be shaken, Your Word will never change. I shall continue until my dying breath to impress Your Word on my children and on their children and on their children because You are the source of all things true and safe and praiseworthy. As they seek to obey Your commands and follow Your ways, they will find true success and the peace that passes understanding. There is no greater thing I can give them than to remind them of Your love and the importance of elevating Your wisdom above their own. I will talk about Your ways at home and at work and when I go places and when I lie down and when I get up. Bless them, protect and guide them and pour Your wisdom into each precious heart. In Jesus' name. Amen.

Proclamation Over Our Family:

In the name of Jesus Christ of Nazareth, I speak knowledge of the ways of the LORD over my family. As for me and my house, we *will* serve the LORD.

Requests

_____
_____
_____
_____
_____
_____

Answers, Changes & Thoughts

_____
_____
_____
_____
_____
_____
_____
_____
_____
_____
_____
_____
_____

Day Twenty-One

Praise: Father God, we run to You in the storms of life. You are our hiding place, a sure refuge in tempestuous times. We rest under Your wing.

Promise: Matthew 7:24, 25 says, "Therefore everyone who hears these words of Mine and puts them into practice is like a wise man who built his house on the rock. The rain came down, the streams rose, and the winds blew and beat against that house; yet it did not fall, because it had its foundation on the rock."

Prayer & Blessing for Our Family:

Father God, there is so much in the news about storms, earthquakes and flooding, all things beyond our control. I pray You will bless and protect our family and give them the wisdom they need for the challenges they face. I pray they will have no fear of the things they can't control, knowing that as they bind themselves to Your heart, they have nothing to fear. I pray their hearts will be open to You as You seek to pour Your wisdom into their minds and spirits. I pray that every one will be firmly planted on You as their foundation and they will have the boldness to share Your critical Word with others. In Jesus' name I pray. Amen.

Proclamation Over Our Family:

In the name of Jesus Christ of Nazareth, I declare salvation and the peace of God over every member of my family.

Requests

_____
_____
_____
_____
_____
_____
_____
_____

Answers, Changes & Thoughts

_____
_____
_____
_____
_____
_____
_____
_____
_____
_____
_____
_____

Day Twenty-Two

Praise: Father God, we give You praise as our source of every good thing.

Promise: Matthew 6:19-21 says, "Do not store up for yourselves treasures on earth, where moth and rust destroy, and where thieves break in and steal. But store up for yourselves treasures in heaven, where moth and rust do not destroy, and where thieves do not break in and steal. For where your treasure is, there your heart will be also."

Prayer & Blessing for Our Family:

Dear LORD, I pray You will send Your angels to minister wherever Your people are today. I pray for safety, good sleep and blessing for every one of my family, and that every one of them will put more thought and energy into storing up treasures in heaven than storing up treasures on earth that they will eventually lose anyway. I pray You will bless us with enough bounty to be able to share with those in need. We know there are so many who are unable to climb into their own beds tonight. Please teach us to value the right things. In Jesus' name. Amen.

Proclamation Over Our Family:

In the name of Jesus Christ of Nazareth, I speak righteousness, faith, safety and provision over my family.

_____

_____

_____

Requests

_____
_____
_____
_____
_____
_____
_____
_____
_____
_____

Answers, Changes & Thoughts

_____
_____
_____
_____
_____
_____
_____
_____
_____
_____
_____
_____
_____
_____

Day Twenty-Three

Praise: O LORD, You are our God; our Father, from whom all things have come; our LORD, Jesus Christ, through whom we live; and our Holy Spirit, through whom we have Your life. We love You.

Promise: Deuteronomy 4:40 says, "Keep His decrees and commands, which I am giving you today, so that it may go well with you and your children after you and that you may live long in the land the LORD you God gives you for all time."

Prayer & Blessing for Our Family:

Father God, thank You for showing us the way and giving us guidelines for life. I pray that my children and their children and their children will love and serve You so that You will be pleased and things will go well with them. LORD, when I look back on our lives, most times of sadness were caused by someone doing something totally out of Your will. LORD, I love my family and I want them to have good, strong, happy, healthy lives. Please, please stir every one to love You so much that they put You first in their lives. Please stir them to be people who tell others about Your great love. In Jesus' name.

Proclamation Over Our Family:

In the name of Jesus, I speak the overflowing love and mercy of God over my family.

Requests

_____
_____
_____
_____
_____
_____
_____
_____
_____
_____

Answers, Changes & Thoughts

_____
_____
_____
_____
_____
_____
_____
_____
_____
_____
_____
_____
_____

Day Twenty-Four

Praise: Father God, we lift our praise to You this day, filling our mouths with words of adoration to You. We worship You as the God of all things and as LORD of our hearts.

Proverb: Proverbs 16:25 says, "There is a way that seems right to a man, but the end of it is the way of death."

Prayer & Blessing for Our Family:

Dear LORD, Your Word says that everyone thinks his or her own way is right because it feels and seems right and appears to makes sense, but You warn about such thinking leading to death. You say there is only one criterion for truth and wisdom, and that is Your will and Your way, as You gave it to us in the Bible. LORD, my prayer for my family is that You would draw every one of them close to Your heart; open their eyes to Your truth; stir them to reach out for Your love. In Jesus' name I pray. Amen.

Proclamation Over Our Family:

In the name of Jesus Christ of Nazareth, I speak truth, salvation and fullness in the Holy Spirit over my entire family.

Requests

_____

_____

_____

_____

_____

Answers, Changes & Thoughts

Day Twenty-Five

Praise: Father God, adoration flows from our hearts. We see You, the Light of the world, seated on Your throne of light and we bow before You, casting our crowns at Your feet.

Promise: Romans 12:2 says, "Do not conform any longer to the pattern of this world, but be transformed by the renewing of your mind. Then you will be able to test and approve what God's will is— His good, pleasing and perfect will."

Prayer & Blessing for Our Family:

Dear LORD, the expectations of this world are generally so contrary to Your guidelines for us. When we feel the inner promptings of Your Holy Spirit nudging us to go Your way, please help us to really do it. Please give each of us the inner strength to dare to step out and please You instead of the world. I pray that we will be people who have the wisdom and individuality to step away from things that make us look "cool" to people and seek to look cool to You instead. Please give us constant reality checks in terms of what is important in order for us to live eternally with You. In Jesus' name I pray. Amen.

Proclamation Over Our Family:

I speak strength, godly character, transformed minds and a passion for knowing the Word of God over every one of my family, in the name of Jesus.

_____

_____

_____

_____

Requests

_____
_____
_____
_____
_____
_____
_____
_____
_____

Answers, Changes & Thoughts

_____
_____
_____
_____
_____
_____
_____
_____
_____
_____
_____
_____
_____

Day Twenty-Six

Praise: Father God, we welcome You into every conversation and give thanks and praise for the presence of Your Holy Spirit with us.

Promise: Hebrews 10:36 says, "You need to persevere so that when you have done the will of God, you will receive what he has promised."

Prayer & Blessing for Our Family:

LORD God, sometimes it's difficult to be consistent and to really persevere in doing Your will. It's easier to do whatever we feel like doing. However, LORD, Your Word admonishes us to persevere in doing Your will because that's the only way we can receive what You have promised. LORD, I pray You will bless us with a supernatural desire to do Your will and we will find no pleasure in going our own way. LORD, I pray that every one of my precious family will be together in the end, receiving what You have promised. I pray not one will be left behind. In Jesus' name. Amen.

Proclamation Over Our Family:

In the name of Jesus Christ of Nazareth, I speak unity over my family. I speak the restoration of family bonds and a fresh valuing of each other. I proclaim harmony where there is disharmony and grace where there is discord.

_____

_____

_____

_____

Requests

_____
_____
_____
_____
_____
_____
_____

Answers, Changes & Thoughts

_____
_____
_____
_____
_____
_____
_____
_____
_____
_____
_____
_____
_____

Day Twenty-Seven

Praise: Father God, we praise and thank You for your unwavering faithfulness. To You, we can entrust our lives, our families and every hope. You alone are worthy.

*Promise:*Proverbs 3:5-6 says, "Trust in the LORD with all your heart and lean not on your own understanding; in all your ways acknowledge him, and he will make your paths straight."

Prayer & Blessing for Our Family:

Dear LORD, please help every one of us trust You with all our hearts. Trusting our own assessments of things is foolish because we don't know all the factors involved, either in specific situations or in this life in general, but You know and see every detail—even the hidden things. Your assessments can be trusted and so we will keep our eyes on You. Please help us remember to acknowledge You in all we do. Thank You in advance for making our paths straight. In Jesus' name we pray. Amen.

Proclamation Over Our Family:

In the name of Jesus Christ of Nazareth, I proclaim this Word of the LORD over my family. As we acknowledge Him, He will make our paths straight.

_____

_____

_____

_____

_____

_____

Requests

_____
_____
_____
_____
_____
_____
_____

Answers, Changes & Thoughts

_____
_____
_____
_____
_____
_____
_____
_____
_____
_____
_____
_____
_____
_____

Day Twenty-Eight

Praise: Father God, we give You praise and thanks for our family. We worship You as our Creator, the One who formed us with divine purpose. We long to bless You.

Promise: Psalm 127:3 says, "Sons are a heritage from the LORD, children a reward from Him."

Prayer & Blessing for Our Family:

Dear LORD, thank You for the family You have given me. My heritage would have meant little without all of them and I am so grateful that You gave each precious one to me. I pray Your greatest blessings on them individually—on (name each family member) ... and all those they love. I pray You will teach all of us Your ways so that we can all be together throughout eternity. In Jesus' Name I pray, amen.

Proclamation Over Our Family:

In the name of Jesus, I speak blessing, salvation and the fullness of the Holy Spirit over each one of my family.

Requests

_____

_____

_____

_____

_____

_____

_____

Answers, Changes & Thoughts

Day Twenty-Nine

Praise: Father God, I offer You the sacrifice of praise. Despite feelings of exhaustion, disappointment or sadness, I lift my praise to You because You are worthy to receive all glory, honour and praise. You are LORD of all my moments, good and sad. You are LORD over all. I trust in You.

Precept: Colossians 1:28, 29 says, "We proclaim Christ, admonishing and teaching our children with all wisdom, so that we may present all of our children perfect in Christ. To this end we labor, struggling with all His energy, which so powerfully works in us (me), their parent(s)."

Prayer & Blessing for Our Family:

LORD, You know I don't always feel like praying, but I cannot give in. Sometimes I feel as though I have no fight left in me. I'm tired and alone. I feeling like giving up. Sometimes I feel like the poster person for Ms or Mr. Misunderstood. Nevertheless, my family has much of Your Word planted in them from a variety of sources. I know, when the time comes and they need You, You will be able to remind them of it—and of Your love for them. And that's the important thing. My greatest hope is that they will all know You. I release them to you. I know You are faithful. In Jesus' name. Amen.

Proclamation Over Our Family:

In the name of Jesus, I speak strength, wholeness, health, faith and blessing over every one of my family.

Requests

_____
_____
_____
_____
_____
_____
_____

Answers, Changes & Thoughts

_____
_____
_____
_____
_____
_____
_____
_____
_____
_____
_____
_____
_____
_____

Day Thirty

Praise: Father God, we wait for You. We wait for You, God Almighty, Prince of Peace. In Your presence, troubles vanish.

Promise: Psalm 46:1-3 says, "God is our refuge and strength, a very present help in trouble. Therefore we will not fear, even though the earth be removed, and though the mountains be carried into the midst of the sea; though its waters roar and be troubled, though the mountains shake with its swelling."

Prayer & Blessing for Our Family:

LORD, You have revealed, and continue to reveal, the strength of our faith in difficult circumstances. Help us to put our trust in You in the midst of transition and chaos. Please motivate us to seek Your face and renew ourselves in devotion and dedication to Your kingdom. These are precarious times and I know we must be established in unwavering faith. LORD, I pray You will bless each of my family with that kind of faith. I pray You will wrap Your arms of grace around them tonight and bless them with Your love and understanding. In Jesus' name I pray. Amen.

Proclamation Over Our Family:

In the name of Jesus, I speak strength and unwavering faith over my family, no matter what the circumstances around them.

Requests

_____
_____
_____
_____
_____
_____
_____

Answers, Changes & Thoughts

_____
_____
_____
_____
_____
_____
_____
_____
_____
_____
_____
_____
_____
_____

Day Thirty-One

Praise: Father God, we enter into Your presence with repentant hearts and praise on our lips—and we wait for You.

Promise: Jeremiah 23:29 says, "'Is not My Word like fire,' declares the LORD, 'and like a hammer that breaks a rock in pieces?'"

Prayer & Blessing for Our Family:

Father God, we need Your Word concerning some of the rubble and huge issues standing in the way of our family restoration. We know that only You can burn away the rubble and break down our issues into bits we can (with Your wisdom) handle. LORD, I see Your Word, like a mighty hammer, smashing apart the huge blocks of resistance in our way. Let it be so, LORD Jesus, in Your holy name. Amen.

Proclamation Over Our Family:

In the name of Jesus Christ of Nazareth, I declare the seemingly insurmountable obstacles in our way turned to dust. Thank You, LORD, for the application of Your Word.

Requests

Answers, Changes & Thoughts

Day Thirty-Two

Praise: Father God, we praise You not just for the blessings You pour out on us but for who You are.

Promise: Deuteronomy 26:11 says, "You shall rejoice in all the good things the LORD your God has given to you and your household."

Prayer & Blessing for Our Family:

Dear LORD, we are grateful for all the good things You have given to us. When we stop to count our blessings, we cannot help but rejoice. We are so blessed to have our freedom and the privilege of living in a democracy. Please make us mindful of whatever we must do to maintain it and stir us to contribute to peace for others. LORD, we pray that the fruit of our lives will have great eternal significance. In Jesus' name we pray. Amen.

Proclamation Over Our Family:

In the name of Jesus Christ of Nazareth, I speak peace, protection, security and blessing over every one of my family.

Requests

_____

_____

_____

_____

_____

Answers, Changes & Thoughts

Day Thirty-Three

Praise: Father God, we love You. We praise You in the midst of our circumstances, whether joyful or challenging. You are LORD.

Precept: Ephesians 5:15-17 says, "Be very careful, then, how you live—not as unwise but as wise, making the most of every opportunity, because the days are evil. Therefore do not be foolish, but understand what the LORD's will is."

Prayer & Blessing for Our Family:

Father God, we know these times are precarious. The instability in the world is huge and we can't be like ostriches hiding our heads in the sand. We must be ready for any eventuality —no matter what it is. We know, LORD, that the only way to be truly prepared is in our hearts. I pray, Father, that You will create clean hearts in every one of us—hearts that are prepared to stand before You in the blink of an eye. I pray for wisdom, LORD, that we will be mindful of things that are truly important and that we will trust Your Word rather than our own ideas because it's only Your ideas that will ensure our true security. Help us to seek Your wisdom rather than our own and to believe Your whole Word, not just the parts that appeal to us. Make us ready to meet You, LORD. In Jesus' name we pray. Amen.

Proclamation Over Our Family:

In the name of Jesus Christ of Nazareth, I speak salvation, wisdom and eternal life over every member of my family.

Requests

_____
_____
_____
_____
_____
_____
_____

Answers, Changes & Thoughts

_____
_____
_____
_____
_____
_____
_____
_____
_____
_____
_____
_____
_____

Day Thirty-Four

Praise: Father God, You are the God of justice and we praise You for Your everlasting kindness and mercy.

Proverb: Proverbs 17:3 says, "The refining pot is for silver and the furnace for gold, but the LORD tests the hearts."

Prayer & Blessing for Our Family:

Dear LORD, thank You for Your great love for us. Thank You for the place You are preparing for us to live with You eternally. We know we are in the process of being refined and sifted to remove all that is coarse so we will be ready to meet You when You return. Sometimes that process seems difficult as we encounter challenge after challenge here on this earth. I pray You will give each of us wisdom, strength, endurance and insight into what You are doing in our lives so we can grow ever closer to You. I pray You will bless each of us with enormous trust in You and total belief in Your Word. I pray we would not be people who get into heaven by the skin of our our teeth. Rather, may You pour Your love through us to gather many people to know and love You. Please help us to be people You can use to bring great glory to You. In Jesus' name we pray. Amen.

Proclamation Over Our Family:

In the name of Jesus Christ of Nazareth, I speak hearts of love, kindness and compassion towards those in need.

_____

_____

_____

Requests

_____
_____
_____
_____
_____
_____
_____

Answers, Changes & Thoughts

_____
_____
_____
_____
_____
_____
_____
_____
_____
_____
_____
_____
_____

Day Thirty-Five

Praise: Father God, You alone are worthy of praise. We magnify Your holy name and love to tell of Your goodness.

Promise: Psalm 78:4 says, "We will not hide them from their children; we will tell the next generation the praiseworthy deeds of the LORD, His power, and the wonders He has done."

Prayer & Blessing for Our Family:

Dear LORD, thank You for all the amazing things You have done for our family. It would be good to keep a journal through the times of difficulty to have a record of Your provision and Your astounding grace as an encouragement for the coming generations as they go through challenges of their own. Please give us ways to share the stories of Your great love for us. Bless each dear one, I pray, LORD, and help them to feel Your arms of love around them wherever they are. Please protect them and draw us together in the unity of Your grace. In Jesus' name. Amen.

Proclamation Over Our Family:

In the name of Jesus, I speak the protection of legions of angels over my family. I speak honour, truth, wisdom and clarity over each one.

Requests

_____

_____

_____

_____

_____

Answers, Changes & Thoughts

Day Thirty-Six

Praise: Father God, we worship You in the golden atmosphere of Your holy presence. We delight in the beauty of singing praises to You. You are everything lovely.

Promise: Psalm 46:1-3 says, "God is our refuge and strength, a very present help in trouble. Therefore we will not fear, even though the earth be removed, and though the mountains be carried into the midst of the sea; though its waters roar and be troubled, though the mountains shake with its swelling."

Prayer & Blessing for Our Family:

Dear LORD, we pray today for the Arabs and the Jews in Israel and Palestine. We pray for the peace of Jerusalem and for revelation of You as the Messiah to all people, all over the world. We pray they will draw close to You, so that no matter what happens here on earth, they will be with You eternally. I pray today You will bless our family and draw every one into a place of safety in Your heart. I pray especially for the parents of little ones, that You will replace any fear from world events with total trust in You and an expectation of wonderful times together in the future. Please give them an understanding of life here as preparation for eternity, and not just as days spent on earth. In Jesus' name I pray. Amen.

Proclamation Over Our Family:

In the name of Jesus, I speak healing, trust, joy, strength and Holy Spirit empowerment over every member of my family.

Requests

_____
_____
_____
_____
_____
_____

Answers, Changes & Thoughts

_____
_____
_____
_____
_____
_____
_____
_____
_____
_____
_____
_____
_____
_____

Day Thirty-Seven

Praise: Father God, when we praise You, our hearts and minds soar beyond this earthly plane into your heart of endless love, warmth and safety. It is here, only here, we know true freedom and peace. It is here all worry drops away, like raindrops falling from a leaf. It is here we bask in the Sonshine of Your grace.

Promise: Jeremiah 29:11-13 says, " For I know the plans I have for you," declares the LORD, "plans to prosper you and not to harm you, plans to give you hope and a future. Then you will call on Me and come and pray to Me, and I will listen to you. You will seek Me and find Me when you seek Me with all your heart."

Prayer & Blessing for Our Family:
Dear LORD, thank You that You have plans to prosper us and not to harm us, plans to give us hope and a future. I pray every one of my family will seek You with all their hearts. Thank You for Your promise that, if they do, they will find You. LORD, I pray my family will have hearts to serve, love and support each other, as well as You. Help them to understand Your plan and purpose for our family. Help them to reconnect Your way. Pour Your love over us and through us. In Jesus' name. Amen.

Proclamation Over Our Family:
In the name of Jesus Christ of Nazareth, I speak prosperity, protection, hope and a godly future over my family.

Requests

_____
_____
_____
_____
_____
_____
_____
_____

Answers, Changes & Thoughts

_____
_____
_____
_____
_____
_____
_____
_____
_____
_____
_____
_____
_____
_____
_____

Day Thirty-Eight

Praise: Sweet adoration flows from our hearts. We give You the highest praise. No words have been formed to express the fullness of love we offer up to You, our Redeemer.

Promise: Isaiah 55:10-11says, "As the rain and the snow come down from heaven, and do not return to it without watering the earth and making it bud and flourish, so that it yields seed for the sower and bread for the eater, so is My Word that goes out from My mouth: It will not return to Me empty, but will accomplish what I desire, and achieve the purpose for which I sent it."

Prayer & Blessing for Our Family:

Dear LORD, thank You for giving us Your Word. Just like the process of photosynthesis, Your Word comes down to us and cycles back up to You, but not without purpose. I pray Your Word will pour over my family and accomplish all You want it to accomplish in each one of us. LORD, You are faithful and so I pray this promise back to You in expectation of Your Word ministering to the hearts of my family. I expect every scripture they have ever heard to return to You, having accomplished something in their hearts. I pray Your purpose will be achieved in each of us. Bless each one, I pray. In Jesus' name. Amen.

Proclamation Over Our Family:

In the name of Jesus, I speak the Word of God over my family and myself. I speak penetration into every cell of our bodies, into our spirits and into our minds.

Requests

_____

_____

_____

_____

_____

_____

_____

Answers, Changes & Thoughts

_____

_____

_____

_____

_____

_____

_____

_____

_____

_____

_____

_____

_____

Day Thirty-Nine

Praise: Father God, You are LORD over all—over our past, our present, our future and our eternity. You are LORD over our desires, our destiny and the details of our lives. We honour You.

Promise: John 15:16 says, "You did not choose Me, but I chose you and appointed you that you should go and bear fruit, and that your fruit should remain, that whatever you ask the Father in My Name, He may give you."

Prayer & Blessing for Our Family:

Dear LORD, thank You so much for answered prayer today. Thank You that You have chosen us for Your special purposes. You have gifted us each individually for the purposes You had in mind when You created us. LORD, I pray that each one of my family would look to You to enter into his or her destiny. I pray there will be great fruit from our lives. I pray blessing on each one and pray You will provide for their every need. I pray for each one individually (name each one) that you will fill them with Your joy, health and provision. I lift up those family members with their own homes, that their homes would be filled with Your presence, peace and the knowledge of You. I pray that You would be loved in each home. In the name of Jesus. Amen.

Proclamation Over Our Family:

In the name of Jesus, I speak the destiny of God into each one of my family. I speak joy into their homes and protection and blessing over each one.

Requests

_____
_____
_____
_____
_____
_____
_____

Answers, Changes & Thoughts

_____
_____
_____
_____
_____
_____
_____
_____
_____
_____
_____
_____
_____
_____

Day Forty

Praise: Father God, we wait for You. We call on Your Name and we wait for You. We wait in worship.

Promise: Psalm 91:15 says, "He shall call upon Me and I will answer him; I will be with him in trouble; I will deliver him and honour him."

Prayer & Blessing for Our Family:

Dear LORD, thank You for Your response to us. The knowledge that You are always here, always ready to communicate with us is so critical. Even when we feel separated from each other, we know You are with us, working in hearts to draw us together in You. Thank You for Your promise that You are always with us in trouble. We never have to go through things alone—and if we take a good look at the situation, we can always find something You are teaching us though it. For those who are having difficulty finding Your presence in their painful circumstances, please help them feel Your arms of love. Thank You for Your promise to deliver us from difficulties and to bring honour to us as we follow You. Please bless our family tonight LORD. Protect and guard each one, I pray. In Jesus' name. Amen.

Proclamation Over Our Family:

In the name of Jesus, I speak wholeness, health and provision over the lives of my family, according to the promises of God.

Requests

_____

_____

_____

_____

_____

_____

_____

Answers, Changes & Thoughts

_____

_____

_____

_____

_____

_____

_____

_____

_____

_____

_____

_____

_____

Day Forty-One

Praise: Jesus, we look to You as the author and finisher of our faith (Hebrews 12:2), the holy One who now sits at the right hand of the throne of God making intercession for us. We praise and thank You for what You have done, and are now doing on our behalf.

Promise: Psalm 37:5 tells us to "Commit your way to the LORD, trust also in Him, and He shall bring it to pass."

Prayer & Blessing for Our Family:

Dear LORD, sometimes it's very difficult to know what way to go or what choices are the right ones in this life. Thank You for Your promise that if we commit our way to You and *trust* in You, You will help us and bring the desires of our hearts to pass. In Psalm 37:23, You say, "The steps of a good man are ordered by the LORD, and He delights in his way." Oh God, I pray that we, individually, would take these verses to heart so that whatever may be muddled in our lives will be righted and we will seek Your direction before making further choices. Thank You that we do not have to rely entirely on our own judgment because we have found it to be flawed. We need Your strength and direction to get through this life well, having fulfilled Your purpose for our lives. In Jesus' name we pray. Amen.

Proclamation Over Our Family:

In the name of Jesus, I speak blessing over my family in whatever areas of need they may have.

Requests

_____
_____
_____
_____
_____
_____
_____
_____

Answers, Changes & Thoughts

_____
_____
_____
_____
_____
_____
_____
_____
_____
_____
_____
_____
_____
_____
_____

Day Forty-Two

Praise: Father God, we praise You as the God of the impossible. Nothing is too hard for You. Your love has no limits. Your will and Your ways are perfect. We trust Your understanding of the things we don't understand.

Promise: Luke 18:27 says, "The things which are impossible with men are possible with God."

Prayer & Blessing for Our Family:

LORD, You know all the places in our hearts and family that need healing and fixing. We lift them up to You, for Your special touch and ministry—because *without* You, we can do nothing about these seemingly impossible situations. But *with* You, nothing is impossible. Thank You for the hope You give us and the faithfulness we have seen and experienced in You. LORD, we are holding out for Your beautiful, finished work. In Jesus' Name we pray, amen.

Proclamation Over Our Family:

In the name of Jesus, I speak the healing oil of the Holy Spirit over my family—over every heart, over every home, over every mind and over every body.

Requests

_____

_____

_____

_____

_____

Answers, Changes & Thoughts

Day Forty-Three

Praise: Father God, You are LORD over everything. We raise our hearts, minds and voices to You, lifting ourselves from the discouragements of life into the glory of Your presence. Thank You for the liberty we find here in You. We cast our cares upon You, knowing You will sustain us.

Promise: Micah 7:8 says, "Do not rejoice over me, my enemy; when I fall, I will rise; when I sit in darkness, the LORD will be a light to me."

Prayer & Blessing for Our Family:

Dear LORD, it is so empowering to know that even when we stumble and fall—or get depressed, or get knocked down by the enemy—that through You, we can get back up and emerge victorious over whatever tried to destroy us. It is so encouraging to know we don't have to be slaves to darkness, depression or discouragement because, in our darkness, You promise to be a light to us. Thank You that You have promised never to leave us or forsake us. In Jesus' name. Amen.

Proclamation Over Our Family:

In the name of Jesus, the Light of the World, I speak His powerful and precious light of life over my family—healing, blessing and restoring.

_____

_____

_____

_____

_____

Requests

_____
_____
_____
_____
_____
_____
_____

Answers, Changes & Thoughts

_____
_____
_____
_____
_____
_____
_____
_____
_____
_____
_____
_____
_____
_____
_____

Day Forty-Four

Praise: Father God, we praise You as the God of purpose, plans and preparation for eternal life with You. You are higher than anything and Your ways are higher than our ways. We praise You for Your infinite grace and wisdom.

Promise: Hebrews 12:11 says, "All discipline for the moment seems not to be joyful but sorrowful; yet to those who have been trained by it, afterwards it yields the peaceful fruit of righteousness."

Prayer & Blessing for Our Family:

Dear LORD, thank you for bringing us through difficult times. Without You, they would have been purposeless, painful and defeating. But through You, we can turn the hard things in our lives around to help other people through life —and sometimes to help them get to know You. You know every circumstance in the lives of every one of my family that is causing pain, turmoil or frustration. I pray You would be with them in the midst of those (often secret) things. Please send Your angels to minister to them in a way that would point them to You, precious LORD. In Jesus' name I pray. Amen.

Proclamation Over Our Family:

In the name of Jesus Christ of Nazareth, I speak fullness of life over my family; that their circumstances wouldn't be empty happenings that toss them to and fro, but that they would be tools in Your hands to draw them closer to You, dear LORD.

Requests

_____

_____

_____

_____

_____

_____

_____

_____

Answers, Changes & Thoughts

_____

_____

_____

_____

_____

_____

_____

_____

_____

_____

_____

_____

_____

Day Forty-Five

Praise: Father God, we praise You as the God of time and eternity. We understand You are not in a rush because You see every strand that has to be spun, strengthened, repaired and renewed for the weaving of our lives. We trust You in all things. We love You, LORD. We love You.

Promise: Isaiah 40:31 says, "They that wait upon the LORD shall renew their strength. They shall mount up on wings as eagles. They shall run and not be weary, they shall walk and not faint."

Prayer & Blessing for Our Family:

Dear LORD, we entrust our family to You. Family was Your idea, Your plan for the organization of society. Ours has been broken by circumstances outside our control. Fixing it isn't in our ability, LORD, so we ask You to please do it. Mend the brokenness and meld our hearts back together, I pray. We know that our timing is not necessarily Your timing because Your ways are higher than ours. You have perfect understanding of all that has to be done in the process—so we will wait and trust. You promise that if we wait on You, You will renew our strength—and so that is what we will do. We wait for You. We love You, LORD. In Jesus' name we pray. Amen.

Proclamation Over Our Family:

In the name of Jesus Christ of Nazareth, I speak total healing, unity, prosperity and peace over my family.

Requests

_____
_____
_____
_____
_____
_____
_____

Answers, Changes & Thoughts

_____
_____
_____
_____
_____
_____
_____
_____
_____
_____
_____
_____
_____
_____

Day Forty-Six

Praise: Father God, we thank You for Your love, compassion, mercy and grace towards us. We praise You, LORD.

Promise: 1 Peter 3:8-9 says, "Finally, all of you, be like-minded, be sympathetic, love one another, be compassionate and humble. Do not repay evil with evil or insult with insult. On the contrary, repay evil with blessing, because to this you were called so that you may inherit a blessing."

Prayer & Blessing for Our Family:

Dear LORD, thank You for showing us how to live together in harmony. I pray our family will be filled with a super abundance of unity, love for one another, sympathy and compassion. I pray there will be no more harshness, bitterness, rancor, mistrust, rejection or pain from family relationships. I pray each family member will have a sense of responsibility in restoring our family and that each one would be thoughtful and seek to bless the others. LORD, I pray our family will be marked by kind hearts and consideration, one for another. Most of all, I pray, LORD, for a great move of Your Holy Spirit over us all, for Your life to indwell every member. In Jesus' name I pray. Amen.

Proclamation Over Our Family:

In the name of Jesus Christ of Nazareth, I speak the love and unity of the Holy Spirit over our family and over each precious one in it.

Requests

_____
_____
_____
_____
_____
_____
_____

Answers, Changes & Thoughts

_____
_____
_____
_____
_____
_____
_____
_____
_____
_____
_____
_____
_____
_____

Day Forty-Seven

Praise: Father God, again we come before You, again offering a sacrifice of praise. No matter how wild this ride of life may be, we come before You and offer our sacrifice of praise, knowing You have a plan we may not see and that Your ways are higher than our ways. We bow before You in simple trust.

Promise: Psalm 112:5-8 says, "A good man deals graciously and lends; he will guide his affairs with discretion. Surely he will never be shaken; the righteous will be in everlasting remembrance. He will not be afraid of evil tidings; his heart is steadfast, trusting in the LORD. His heart is established; he will not be afraid..."

Prayer & Blessing for Our Family:

Father God, we know You have called us to quiet our souls and keep our emotions under control. It is foolish to allow our circumstances to dictate our sense of well-being. Please help us guide our affairs with discretion. We so often allow disappointment and frustration to take us out of the flow of Your Holy Spirit and remove us from the peace of Your presence. Life often seems like a roller-coaster ride of ups and downs. Please strengthen us to remain solid in our faith and trust in You. Help us to be strong and steady. In Jesus' name.

Proclamation Over Our Family:

In the name of Jesus Christ of Nazareth, I take authority over the circumstances that seek to wreak havoc on our family. I speak the peace of the LORD Jesus Christ over every circumstance.

Requests

_____
_____
_____
_____
_____
_____
_____

Answers, Changes & Thoughts

_____
_____
_____
_____
_____
_____
_____
_____
_____
_____
_____
_____
_____

Day Forty-Eight

Praise: Father God, as we lift our praises to You, we wrap them around every burden we carry. May our praises reach Your heart. May every ache and earthy worry dissolve in Your grace, love, provision and power.

Promise: Matthew 11:28 says, "Come to me, all you who are weary and burdened, and I will give you rest."

Prayer & Blessing for Our Family:

Father God, please help us lay all our challenges at Your feet and enter into Your rest, stop worrying and trust that You are working out the complications of our lives. Thank You for Your promise of rest if we will just spend time in Your presence. I pray Your blessing of rest—sweet rest—over my family. In Jesus' name I pray. Amen.

Proclamation Over Our Family:

In the Name of Jesus Christ of Nazareth, I speak rest to the hearts and souls of each one of my precious family as they spend time in Your presence.

Requests

_____

_____

_____

_____

_____

_____

Answers, Changes & Thoughts

Day Forty-Nine

Praise: Father God, You are the God of all eternity. We worship You with awe and adoration, waiting to be with You—forever.

Promise: 2 Corinthians 4:18 says, "So we fix our eyes not on what is seen, but on what is unseen, since what is seen is temporary, but what is unseen is eternal."

Prayer & Blessing for Our Family:

Father God, our eyes are fixed on Your eternal, individual purpose for each of us. We are beyond grateful to know You are at work in the lives of those for whom we are praying, drawing their hearts so they will be saved from eternal torment. We pray Your eternal blessing on our entire family—and not just for our own eternal comfort—but so we will all have a passion to reach out to lost people everywhere with Your grace, mercy, forgiveness and acceptance. In Jesus' name. Amen.

Proclamation Over Our Family:

In the name of Jesus Christ of Nazareth, I speak the eternal blessing of the LORD over every one who will turn his or her heart over to Him.

Requests

_____

_____

_____

_____

_____

Answers, Changes & Thoughts

Day Fifty

Praise: Father God, we praise and worship You as the Almighty Warrior King who will do battle for us in situations beyond our control.

Promise: 2 Chronicles 20:15 says, "Listen, King Jehoshaphat and all who live in Judah and Jerusalem! This is what the LORD says to you: 'Do not be afraid or discouraged because of this vast army. For the battle is not yours, but God's.'"

Prayer & Blessing for Our Family:

Father God, thank You for the stories of Your supernatural intervention in situations many generations ago. Sometimes the challenges we face seem overwhelming and we can't do anything to fix them. Because You are the God who never changes, we know You can intervene for us now in the same way you intervened for our forefathers. Please help us lay our worry and striving down and simply trust in You to accomplish Your purposes in our lives. We pray You will bless us with victory over every hindering spirit that would seek to destroy our family. In Jesus' name. Amen.

Proclamation Over Our Family:

In the name of Jesus Christ of Nazareth, I speak the blessing of God's victory into the lives of my family.

Requests

_____

_____

_____

_____

Answers, Changes & Thoughts

Day Fifty-One

Praise: Father God, We worship and wait for You.

Promise: 2 Chronicles 20:17 says, "You will not have to fight this battle. Take up your positions; stand firm and see the deliverance the LORD will give you, ... Do not be afraid; do not be discouraged. Go out to face them tomorrow, and the LORD will be with you."

Prayer & Blessing for Our Family:

Father God, we stand before You, waiting to see the deliverance You will bring if we take up the positions You have given us and stand firm. We will not waver in our expectation of Your victory over our circumstances. We take authority over all spirits of fear and discouragement in the name of Jesus. We thank you in advance for blessing us with Your victory.

Proclamation Over Our Family:

In the name of Jesus Christ of Nazareth, I speak victory over every weapon that has been formed against our family for our destruction. I speak the freedom, protection and direction of the Holy Spirit of God.

Requests

_____

_____

_____

_____

_____

Answers, Changes & Thoughts

Day Fifty-Two

Praise: Father God, we worship You as the God of our hope and our salvation. You are the heart of everything good for which we long.

Promise: Isaiah 60:4 says, "Lift up your eyes and look about you: All assemble and come to you; your sons come from afar, and your daughters are carried on the hip."

Prayer & Blessing for Our Family:

LORD God, we see with eyes of faith the eternal assembly of all those we love. Thank You for mending broken hearts, for restoring hope and unity, and for giving us eyes of faith to see the finale of Your amazing work in our lives.

"The LORD bless you and keep you; the LORD make His face shine on you and be gracious to you; the LORD turn His face toward you and give you peace" (Numbers 6:22-26).

Proclamation Over Our Family:

In the name of Jesus Christ of Nazareth, I declare the restoration of godly unity in our family.

Requests

Answers, Changes & Thoughts

Summary
How I've Changed through This Process

When we pray for God to work in the lives of others, what we may not realize is that He really wants to make changes in our lives as well. When the workers completed the walls of Jerusalem, it goes without saying they would have gained strength from all their hard work. In what ways do you feel you have changed through this process of prayer?

_____

_____

_____

_____

_____

_____

_____

_____

_____

_____

_____

_____

_____

_____

_____

_____

_____

_____

_____

Summary

Changes I've Seen in My Family

2 Corinthians 6:2: *"For He says, 'In the time of My favor I heard you, and in the day of salvation I helped you. I tell you, now is the time of God's favor, now is the day of salvation.'"*

8

Dedication & Celebration

Congratulations! You have been faithful through 52 days of prayer for the restoration of your family. It's time to go back to page 55 where you listed your greatest hopes for this *Family Blessing Initiatve* and assess what changes have been made.

Nehemiah's wall was completed on the 25th of Elul, in 52 days. His enemies were upset because they realized the work-had been done with the help of God. The changes in your family will be a wonderful testimony to the skeptics and scoffers who have known what you have been doing.

After taking stock of what had been accomplished, Nehemiah put safeguards in place to protect the work that had been done—as we must do.

Josephus, the historian, records[1] the rebuilding as taking place over a period of two years and four months. This extra time included the additional tasks, such as further strengthening of various sections of the wall and embellishing and beautifying certain areas.

This is important to note because, again, it sets a pattern for the ongoing strengthening of our families. These 52 days of prayer were preliminary to the continuous investment of

1. Antiquities, 11.5.8

time, prayer and attention we must invest in our families. They are lifelong "projects." Families are living organisms; they need to be nurtured, loved, tended and made to feel precious every day of your life.

Let's Have a Party!

The dedication of the wall of Jerusalem was an occasion for a great party. There were choirs, all kinds of instruments and colourful dancing. The sounds of rejoicing could be heard, "far away" because God had given them "great joy."

Even the tiniest steps of restoration will cause great joy. I (Diane) have been hugely encouraged over what happened in my 52 days. My heart is happy. There is still work to be done, but there will always be more to be done. That's life. But for now I am happy because I have seen God do great things and I am looking forward to what else He has in store. I am actually about to embark on a second 52 days.

We (Val and Brenda), surrounded by our family, have experienced the sustaining power of God as we have continued to battle Val's cancer. It was during these 52 days that I (Val) experienced the actual collision of life and death (see p. 33-34) and was given profound insight into the reality of the effects of prayer. I believe this was to give you encouragement to never give up praying—because when you pray, things are really happening in the Holy Spirit realm.

As you mark the end of this 52 days, you might want to do what the Israelites did and have a party to celebrate all that God has done. Dedicate your family to Him, to be used for His purposes, and celebrate.

God's Further Work
in Our Family

_____

_____

_____

_____

_____

_____

_____

_____

_____

_____

_____

_____

_____

_____

_____

_____

_____

_____

_____

_____

Postlogue

We are very sad that Rev. Val Dodd passed away just prior to the printing of this book. We thank God for the vision He gave to him for this *Family Blessing Initiative* and pray it will be a great blessing to you and your family.

To contact Brenda Dodd:

brenda@familyblessinginitiative.org

www.familyblessinginitiative.org

To contact Diane Roblin-Lee:

diane@bydesignmedia.ca

www.bydesignmedia.ca

"There are no institutions that are more important than the home. Building strong families will build a strong nation. There is no doubt it is around the family and the home that all the greatest virtues, the most dominating virtues of human society, are created, strengthened and maintained."

Sir Winston Churchill

CPSIA information can be obtained
at www.ICGtesting.com
Printed in the USA
LVHW031125210819
628380LV00007B/82

9 781896 213729